THE KNOT BOOK

1200
Sterling

THE KNOT BOOK

Geoffrey Budworth

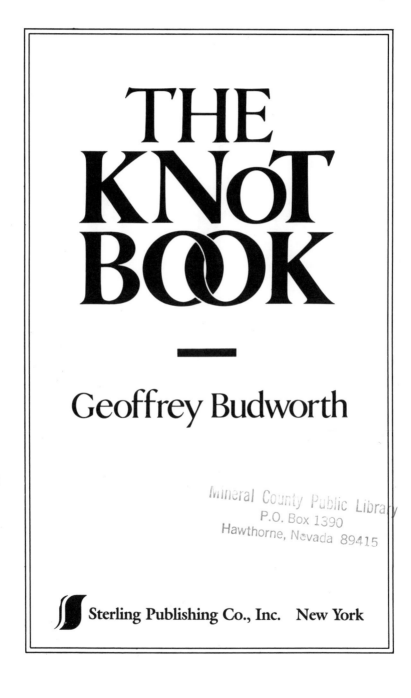

Sterling Publishing Co., Inc.   New York

Dedication

To James Nicoll from Largo in the Kingdom of Fife, still the best knotsman I've ever met, for his friendship and knowledge.

Library of Congress Cataloging in Publication Data

Budworth, Geoffrey.
  The knot book.

  Includes index.
  1. Knots and splices.   I. Title.
VM533.B83   1985   623.88'82   84-26843

ISBN 0-8069-7944-5

First published in Great Britain Copyright Elliot Right Way Books MCMLXXXIII
American edition published in 1985 by Sterling Publishing Co., Inc.
387 Park Avenue South, New York, N.Y. 10016
Distributed in Canada by Oak Tree Press Ltd.
% Canadian Manda Group, P.O. Box 920, Station U
Toronto, Ontario, Canada M8Z 5P9
Manufactured in the United States of America
All rights reserved

Contents

Illustrations

Acknowledgments

No one can be totally original on knots: too many others have drawn and written about them. I gratefully acknowledge all those sources from which I have—consciously or unconsciously—acquired my knotting know-how.

My thanks go to Mr. J. C. Bates of British Ropes Ltd., for bringing together publisher and author; and to Mr. Peter Manners, the manager for the works committee, for his time and encouragement.

A number of friends within the International Guild of Knot Tyers have kindly given me permission to use their original ideas, which I am pleased to portray and describe in print for the first time. I am especially indebted to Canadian climber and guide Bob Chisnall. My knowledge of climbers' knots was largely learned from him. He is also a clever knotting innovator. The Double Hedden Knot is his variation of an established knot. Hunter's Loop, the Adjustable Knot and the Three Quarter Figure of Eight Loops are further examples of his inventiveness. The Double Munter Friction Hitch (which may also be called a Double Crossing Knot) is recommended as a climbers' knot but so far only infrequently adopted by them. His Ontario and Algonquin Bowlines are experiments—not in general climbing use—and (it should be noted) may be regarded as new knots.

It's hard to choose from the many knots by Desmond Mandeville, but I unhesitatingly introduce his Tumbling Thief Knot to the knotting scene, together with the Poor Man's Pride and also Bend "X." Ettrick W. Thomson has contributed his method of tying the Poor Man's Pride.

Others to whom I am indebted for their own original material are my younger daughter Julie for Julie's Hitch; Mr. John Sweet, lifelong scout, knotting writer and authority on pioneering with ropes and spars, for his modification of the Waggoner's Hitch with a strop; and Amory B. Lovins (who pointed out to me the real origin of Hunter's Bend while working in Britain with Friends of the Earth Ltd.) for his Vibration Proof Hitch.

I gratefully acknowledge the generosity of Mr. Spike Milligan for permission to reproduce his apt poem "String" at the beginning of Chapter 4. This poem originally appeared in *Silly Verse for Kids* by Spike Milligan, published by Penguin Books Ltd. (1959).

My sincere thanks also go to Malcolm Elliot for his patience and editorial guidance; and to James Lester, illustrator, for his skill and tenacity in coping with my original drawings.

Introduction

"It is extraordinary how little the average individual knows about the art of making even the simplest knots."—R. M. Abraham, 1932

Imagine you are trapped on an upper floor of a burning building, too high to jump without serious injury. You can improvise a rope by tying bedsheets together, and climb down them. But what knot should you use to tie those bedsheets together?

Have you ever tied an awkward load onto the luggage rack of your car, only to have it shift dangerously after just a few miles? Do you continually stop to retie your shoelaces? Is it difficult to restring a musical instrument or tie up a package? Then you need to know the right knots.

We all have to fasten string or bandages sooner or later; and it's knots that make them work. Housewives, hobbyists, gardeners and modelmakers all use different knots. Whether you are a parent trying to amuse children at a party or a backpacker on a hike, knots will help. You can learn to tie them at any age. One of the knots in this book was invented by a nine-year-old girl; others by a grandfather. Acquiring skill with knots can be good therapy for the sick and the mentally or physically handicapped, or simply an absorbing pastime for anyone.

Many people cope for a long time without knowing any really useful knots, but only because they can replace them with handy manufactured fastenings like safety pins, clasps, snaplinks, screws, glue and those elastic cords with metal hooks on the ends. These items are fine when they're available—I use them all the time—but without them you're lost, unless you can tie a knot or two. Knots are a useful alternative in many circumstances and indispensable in others. That's why so many practical people scorn spending money unnecessarily on gadgets, and take pride in knowing the right knot for the job.

You don't have to like boats to enjoy knotting. Knot books tend to have a nautical flavor, but that is only because old-time seamen did more than any other group to develop practical knotting. Thus, many knots and knotting terms have to do with ships and sailors. Don't be put off by that. The knots are just as useful ashore as they are afloat.

There are thousands of knots and an infinite number of variations of some of them. This book shows you about 100. The first half dozen or so are invaluable, used around the world by everyone who has to make rope, cord or string work for them. The wider selection that follows—including the special knots used by rock climbers and anglers—are all very useful on occasions. Knots are like tools. You can't have too many; then you can always pick just the right one for the job.

(Incidentally, to tie those bedsheets together and escape the fire, learn the Double Sheet Bend, the Fisherman's Knot or the Surgeon's Knot.)

How To Use This Book

The Table of Contents at the beginning of this book will show you where to look for a history of ropemaking, techniques and terms, basic knots, string knots, more general knots, anglers' knots, climbers' knots and other knots as well.

A list of illustrations can be found on pages 8 and 9. If you know the name of a knot or a technique and want to see what it looks like, run your eye quickly down this list to spot the page you need.

If you know roughly what you want to achieve, but don't know the right knot for the job, look at the "Knots According To Use" on page 15, which shows what knot to use for every purpose, from attaching a line to a rail, post or to another line to tying multiple loop knots in the ends of lines for rescuing, salvaging and more.

It's often impractical to deal with every bit of information about one knot before going on to another, so when you find a knot you can use, look it up in the "Knots According To Use" section or in the Index. There may be another mention of it elsewhere. Several similar knots may all do more or less the same job. It can be worth trying two or three. You might find you remember one more easily than the others, or one knot may work better than the others depending on what your rope is made of. For this reason, an effort has been made to include a number of alternatives.

All the knotting terms are fully explained as you go along, and they also appear in a Glossary at the end of the book.

Knots
According To Use

KNOTS FOR JOINING THE ENDS OF LINES TOGETHER

KNOTS FOR ATTACHING A LINE TO A RAIL, POST, ANOTHER LINE, ETC.

KNOTS TIED IN THE END OF LINES AS STOPPER KNOTS

BINDING KNOTS

SINGLE LOOP KNOT IN THE END OF LINE

*Note: * means knots are sliding loops which may be adjusted to size*

1 • ALL ABOUT ROPE

HISTORY

Cavemen tied knots. So did the Incas of Peru, who used knotted strings instead of written figures to do complicated bookkeeping. Those knotted strings may be man's oldest tool. Primitive peoples from Eskimos to South Pacific Indians needed knots, and the Ancient Persians, Greeks and Romans probably knew as much about knots as we do.

The Egyptians also knew a great deal about knots. A large 3-strand rope, as well made as many manufactured today, was discovered in the underground limestone quarries of Turah, near Cairo. The rope had probably been used to haul stone for the building of the Great Pyramids of Gizeh and Memphis. The Egyptians were great ropemakers, and they valued rope highly. One of the treasures discovered by archaeologists in the tomb of Tutankhamun was a neatly coiled and braided rope.

The Egyptians were not the first ropemakers, however. The Peruvian Incas made fiber ropes into primitive suspension bridges, while the North American Indians went whale hunting with lines four or five inches in circumference as strong as Manila fiber but four times longer lasting in water.

Knots were also important to the Venetians, who maintained their empire by maritime strength, and in the Middle Ages knotting also acquired religious symbolism and superstitions. Charlatans were punished for "knot sorcery." Renaissance genius Leonardo da Vinci designed a knotted fringe on the gown of the Mona Lisa.

By the 18th century, when every clipper ship was a spider web of rope rigging, illiterate seamen were producing masterpieces of knotted and braided ropework that were both practical and decorative. When commercial sailing ships died, knotting seemed to die out, too.

But people today still need knots. Rock climbers and spelunkers (those who study and explore caves) depend on nylon ropes that have to be knotted. Anglers—like climbers—are concerned with knot strength, but they tie the knots in monofilaments (single plies of man-made fiber). Boating buffs preserve the knots of the old seafarers, but tie them in modern braided ropes. Fishermen continue to make and mend nets.

Some archers still make their own bowstrings. Bookbinders, shoemakers and falconers all use a knot or two in their professions. For firemen, riggers (in the circus and the theater), steeplejacks and stevedores, knots are the tools of their trade. Weavers, river workers and sail-makers keep this knowledge about knots alive, and so do scouts and rangers. Truck drivers may use the Waggoner's Hitch, and we all need to tie shoelaces.

Some people find tying complicated knots as fascinating as any other sort of puzzle. Advanced math students may even study "knot theory," a sort of three-dimensional geometry. Designers use knot patterns to sell items as varied as book jackets, paper plates, dress fabrics and bathing suits.

HOW ROPE IS CONSTRUCTED

Find out for yourself how rope is constructed (Fig. 1).

Examine a short length of 3-strand rope. Hold it vertically. See how the strands move upwards and to the right? That rope is "laid" (twisted) right-handed; 3-strand rope generally is. Left-handed rope is a rarity and, in my experience, usually consists of four strands. Three strands are stronger than four. In addition, using four or more strands (the French have a 6-strand rope) creates an unfilled space that runs like a tunnel through the center of the rope. This space must be filled with a heart (core) of cheap material.

Now uncoil one strand of your piece of rope. The remaining two strands will continue to cling together, held securely by an invisible force, and there will be a clearly defined furrow into which you could replace the absent strand, if you wanted to.

Which way is the separated strand laid up? It's left-handed, spiralling opposite to the whole rope. This is the vital principle of traditional ropemaking. That opposing twist between strands and rope is what actually holds those other two strands together. To replace the third strand successfully, you must not only lay it neatly into the empty right-handed spiral groove, but also give it a left-handed twist at the same time.

Before you try that, separate out one of the yarns which make up the strand. When you remove it, you'll leave a spiral gap, and because there are many yarns in a strand, it's hard to replace it perfectly. Yarns are, of course, laid up right-handed, opposite to their strands.

Finally, each yarn is loosely spun from thin fibers (or filaments), and these are the basic units of construction of any rope. Monofilaments will run the length of the line and not vary in thickness. Natural vegetable fibers can be only as long as the plant that produced them. Such fibers, graded for size and quality, are known as "staples," and they have the irregularities of any natural product. It is all those projecting staple ends that make a fiber rope "hairy," and the lack of them which makes a synthetic rope smooth. However, if fuzziness is desirable, synthetic filaments can be chopped to staple lengths prior to spinning.

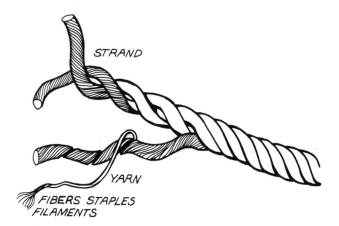

Fig. 1 Rope's construction
Right hand, hawser-laid 3-strand rope.

Vegetable (Natural) Fiber Ropes

Primitive peoples twisted crude but very strong rope from roots, sinew or gut. The Vikings used the skin of sea mammals. Ancient Egyptians worked with papyrus—the reed from which they also produced parchment-like paper—for thousands of years to make rope.

Around 1271 Marco Polo wrote that some Persian vessels were tied together by "a kind of yarn made from coconut fibers." And in 1620 the English explorer George Weymouth reported that Indians whaling along the coast of Maine used "a rope which they make great and strong of Bark of Trees."

Rawhide was braided into lassoes and harnesses by cowboys, who even laboriously wove watch chains with the hair from their horses' tails.

Vegetable fiber rope was used until World War II. During all those centuries the most common fibers remained Manila, sisal; coir (made from coconuts) and hemp. Others included jute and raffia, and even wool and silk.

Ropemakers obtained their raw materials from all over the world. Manila came from the Philippines; hemp from Italy and Russia. Sisal (named after a small port on the Yucatan peninsula) came from Java, Tanzania and Kenya; coir came from the Malabar coast and Sri Lanka (Ceylon). There was Egyptian and American cotton, flax from New Zealand, and esparto grass from Spain and North Africa as well as India, China, Japan and the West Indies.

When political upheaval, civil unrest or war interfered with trade, ropemakers were forced to get their materials elsewhere. The Crimean War of the mid-1800's caused the supply of Russian hemp to fail, which compelled the trade to turn from the soft, flexible fibers used exclusively until that time to hard Manila hemp from the Far East.

Manila hemp proved superior in so many ways that it quickly became the most important cordage material—until 1941, when World War II events cut off Manila. Once more ropemakers were driven to seek a new solution. The answer was to make rope from synthetic materials. This was the biggest breakthrough in a thousand years. True, around 1831 iron wire ropes were used in the silver mines of Hungary and Austria. But in 1960 men were still proud that a 2-inch whaleline could withstand the strain of a few hundred pounds. By 1960 nylon climbing ropes of a similar size could withstand over 4,000 pounds.

Natural fiber ropes always had many disadvantages. They swelled and weakened when wet, jamming the knots tied in them and breaking more easily. They rotted, mildewed, and decayed. They were attacked by sun, weather and chemicals. Their strength-to-weight ratio was low, making them enormously bulky, requiring large storage spaces. While they could be cruel on the hands of sailors at any time, they were especially treacherous when they froze like spiky iron bars.

Nevertheless, there is nostalgia in the feel, smell and the evocative names of the old ropes: Italian tarred hemp (the best there was), Egyptian cotton (immaculate for rich men's yachts), brown and hairy coir from coconut husks, and golden fuzzy sisal. Who knows, as we become increasingly concerned about depleting our world's finite resources, it might make sense one day to return to growing renewable ropemaking crops.

Synthetic Ropes

These days ropemakers no longer send to exotic ports for plants, but instead to the laboratories for synthetic fibers. Nylon, polyester and polypropylene are today's main rope materials. You can think of their respective strengths in the proportion of 5:4:3.

Most synthetics originate from oil, but nylon—which comes from coal—is the strongest and most elastic. Its ability to absorb shock-loading by stretching makes it ideal for climbing, towing and mooring.

Polyester is strong too, but not as strong as nylon; nor does it have much stretch, and pre-stretching during its manufacture can remove even that. It is particularly suited for standing rigging and similar jobs where slackness could be inconvenient or even disastrous.

Polypropylene is the least strong of the three, but it's cheaper, so you can buy it thicker, and it floats—an advantage when it is used for lifelines and boating.

Polyethylene, another major product, is relatively weak and waxy to the touch. Cheap yet attractive, it has its uses. Many other substances can be shredded, combed and spun: even celluloid film has been made into rope.

Today's man-made ropes are superb. Whether twisted strands or (increasingly) plaited or braided, there is one for every purpose. Massive mooring ropes for supertankers may be made of one giant plaited rope covered by an even larger plaited rope, braid over braid. Climbers' ropes combine strength, flexibility and lightness through a core of elastic filaments tightly enclosed inside a neatly woven sheath. Weavers and other craftsmen can buy a variety of small cords and yarns, while for tough jobs on industrial sites, or in the garden, there are cruder and cheaper products. Ropemakers will make ropes for special purposes, such as a diver's lifeline, which incorporates a telephone cable. They can even create man-made ropes that imitate the old natural fiber ropes in color, texture and handling qualities.

Synthetic ropes have high tensile strength and exceptional sustained load performance. They have an outstanding capacity to absorb shock-loading, immunity to rot, mildew and marine decay. They resist chemical attack, weathering, and can withstand contact with oils, gasoline and common solvents. Because of their low water absorption, their breaking strain remains constant when wet (vegetable fiber strength decreases 30–40 per cent when wet).

Man-made ropes are easy to handle—wet or dry—and their soft texture won't damage highly finished surfaces. They are lightweight, easy to carry and store, and they have a high strength-to-weight ratio. Those that float do so indefinitely, while all have excellent aging properties, durability and long life.

Colors range from white to black, with reds, oranges, blues and greens also available. Color coding of sheets and halyards (ropes and tackle) on yachts and dinghies is now established practice in the sailing world.

Thanks to the ropemakers, macramé hobbyists and other craftworkers can often produce work of outstanding quality, and the backyard mechanic can tuck a towrope and block-and-tackle into one corner of his toolbox.

The big snag with man-made rope and cordage is its smoothness. Some trusted old knots slip undone when they're tied in synthetic rope. This should be kept in mind. Such knots may need an extra Half Hitch or tuck to secure them.

Synthetic ropes also melt when heated. Even the friction of

one part of the rope rubbing across another may heat it so that it weakens and fails. It's important to avoid any sort of sawing action between rope parts or, as the knot tightens up under a load, the binding of one against another. These actions may actually fuse them all together—never again to be untied. This property of synthetic rope does not need to be a great hazard or inconvenience, but it must be taken into account—especially by climbers and spelunkers.

2 · TECHNIQUES AND TERMS

The best way to learn knots is to have someone who can tie them show you how. But sooner or later, most of us have to teach ourselves knotting from a book. And that's not so easy. You may not be able to follow the step-by-step drawings, or the written explanations may confuse you. We all have the same difficulty. So don't be discouraged. Keep trying and you'll soon get the knack of working from drawings to tie real knots.

A Lesson to Remember

The poet John Masefield wrote a hilarious salty yarn about the redheaded and ambitious Jimmy Hicks. Jimmy tied an extra hitch on all his knots, always doing more than was required of him. Ultimately, his ship and all aboard were lost when she foundered in a cyclone because Jimmy took too long rigging the line to launch the lifeboat. The moral of this cautionary tale: Don't be either redheaded or ambitious, and *always use the simplest knot, bend or hitch that will serve your purpose.*

NAMES AND USES

It's no use putting lists of uses and users alongside each knot. Such lists would be long and repetitive, and would still leave too much out. Instead, read carefully what a knot is designed to do. If, say, it's a hitch to attach a rope to a rail or post or another rope, then think about whether you ever need to do that. It makes no difference whether you're a farmer tethering livestock or a windsurfer securing the sail-boom to the mast. If it's the hitch for you, use it. (See "Knots According To Use," page 15.)

Knotting isn't difficult. Children can master many complicated knots as readily as grown-ups. But neither is it always

simple. If it were, it might not be so satisfying. You have to try—
and if it doesn't go right the first time—try again.

HOW ROPE IS DESCRIBED

Handling rope and tying it in knots is easier if you know what
the different parts of the rope are called. The "working end," the
"standing part," the "standing end," a "loop" and a "bight" are
all shown in Fig. 2 and explained in the Glossary.

The term Round Turn needs explanation. When a line completely encircles an object (a post or a rail or another rope) and
the two parts of the resulting loop cross, you have "taken a
turn." But only when you take the end around a *second* time is it
a Round Turn (Fig. 3). The number of Round Turns you have is
always one less than the number of rope parts you *see* encircling
the foundation.

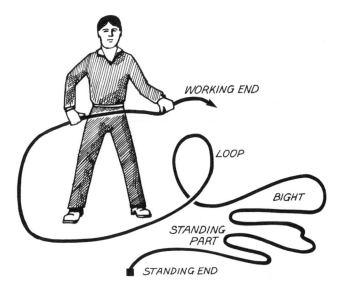

Fig. 2 Rope parts

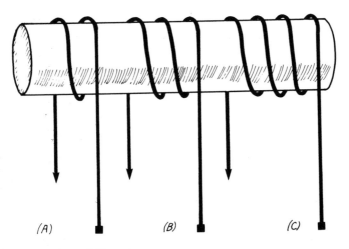

(A)   (B)   (C)

Fig. 3 Round Turns
(A) A Round Turn.
(B) 2 Round Turns.
(C) 3 Round Turns.

KEY TO DRAWINGS

The drawings in this book show all knots in a single line—thick or thin. The working end of the rope is shown with an arrow. The standing end is shown with a black square to signify a load, weight or strain. The exceptions: knots tied "in the bight" (the slack part of the rope), such as the Sheepshank (Fig. 21) where there is no real working end; and binding knots, such as the Transom Knot (Fig. 22) where there is no distinct load end.

Drawings that use a double line show the working end whipped (whipping is the tight wrapping of the end of the rope to prevent its fraying).

The knot diagrams have been drawn in an open layout so that you can see how and where the strands cross over or under one another. The lead—the path taken by the working end—is indicated when necessary, so that you can copy the tying process.

All the knots should be tightened (see "Tightening Knots," page 41). They are drawn in an open layout because it isn't usually much help to see a diagram of the finished knot drawn up snug and tight with all the slack removed. But where the finished knot takes on a totally different shape from the form in which it's tied, the book will point it out or show it in a drawing.

TOOLS

You can learn and practice simple knots without any tools other than your own fingers and some soft, flexible line. Two one-yard lengths of braided white cotton rope (sometimes called magicians' cord or banding) or a synthetic equivalent are ideal. Climbers' long round boot laces (you can find them in sporting goods stores) are also good. Tying complicated knots, however, is always easier when you have the right tools; sometimes it is impossible without one or more of the following:

1.   *a spike*—to force open gaps into which you can tuck working ends, and to open tight knots. Large metal spikes are called "marline spikes." Smaller ones with wooden handles are "prickers," and wooden ones are called "fids." You can buy spikes from yachting suppliers or shops.

2.   *a knife*—*also scissors, shears, snips, pliers, clippers, razor blades* (in a safe holder), and so on, for cutting and trimming everything from single fibers to large cables.

3.   *round-nose pliers*—which help you draw slack rope through when tightening knots. Two pairs, one large and the other small (sometimes called jeweler's pliers) will cope with any task. You can get them at a hardware store.

4.   *wire loops* (Fig. 4)—must be homemade (you can't buy them) from piano wire bent double and inserted into handles so the wire loops won't pull out. Wire loops are *the* single most useful tools for knot tyers. You use them to tug working ends through partially tightened knots, to bury ends, and so on. Make several wire loops of varying lengths and of a couple of different thicknesses of wire.

Fig. 4 A homemade wire loop

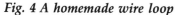

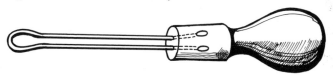

HOW TO TIE A KNOT FROM A DRAWING

Let's take as an example the Packer's Knot (Fig. 5). Locate the "standing end" of the line in the diagram and run your eye along

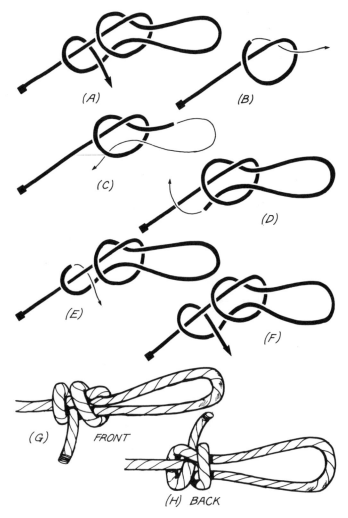

Fig. 5 How to tie a knot from a drawing
(A) Drawing of a Packer's Knot.   (G) Completed knot (front view).
(B)-(F) Stages in tying.   (H) Completed knot (rear view).

the line, over and under at the crossing points (the points where line crosses line) and around the bends, until you arrive at the working end (the one with the arrow). This is the way you will tie the knot.

Now take your piece of string or cord and, using about a foot of it, lay it down like the standing end of the drawing. Bend the working end around and make the first crossing point (Fig. 5B), making sure you go *over* if the drawing indicates *over*. The over-and-under sequence must come out right. Continue to follow the drawing step-by-step (Fig. 5C-F), crossing point by crossing point. Draw the completed knot tight and snug (Fig. 5G-H).

Of course, with practice you'll develop an eye for shortcuts. You'll note that this Packer's Knot is merely a Slip Knot (Fig. 19D) reinforced with a Half Hitch. So, eventually, you'll simply glance at the drawing of a Packer's Knot, identify it, and—in a couple of quick and easy movements—tie a Slip Knot and add a Half Hitch.

Meanwhile, however, use the working end of your line as you would a pencil, drawing a copy of the knot diagram until you have reproduced it accurately in string or cord.

KNOT STRENGTH

Knots weaken rope. The sharper the curve, the tighter the nip (the binding, frictional pressure within the knot that keeps it from slipping), the greater the chance that the rope will break. If it does, it separates immediately outside the knot.

Many traditional knots are surprisingly harmful to the rope they're tied in. The worst offender is the simple Overhand Knot (Fig. 9A), with a breaking strain 40 per cent of the rope's actual strength. Anglers casting with rod and line often unintentionally create this knot in mid air (they call it a Wind knot). If it is not spotted and untied, but allowed to pull tight, it will reduce the breaking strain of the fishing line to less than half!

At the top of the efficiency list come hitches where a Round Turn or two is taken with the line on some foundation—a wide rail or spar, for example—before any tying takes place. The Clove Hitch (breaking strain 75 per cent, Fig. 16) and the Fisherman's Bend (breaking strain 75 per cent, Fig. 17D) are good examples. In these knots the load is absorbed gradually by friction in the turns.

So, you need to choose your knots with care—another reason for knowing several different types. Strong knots are vital to climbers, who use bulky ones with lots of wrapping turns devised to absorb strain and avoid weakening the nylon ropes unnecessarily. They are also crucial to anglers, who use similar (but miniature) barrel-shaped Blood knots in their lines to improve their chances of a catch and prevent the loss of expensive tackle. And they're no less important to family motorists who could be prosecuted for damages if articles on the luggage rack get loose and fall onto the highway. All of us need to know how to tie good knots.

Splices (the interweaving of strands of rope) are stronger than knots and, theoretically, should be used in preference to them wherever possible. Certainly don't use knots on lifting equipment such as cranes. However, while splices can be 90 per cent efficient, they take longer to make than knots, are semi-permanent and limit the rope's uses, leaving it forever distorted and possibly weakened. Splices are not covered in this book, but many excellent pamphlets about them are put out by ropemakers. Ask for one when you buy their products.

A number of modern anglers' knots are 80 per cent, 90 per cent, even 95 per cent efficient, and one unique creation—the Bimini Twist (Fig. 41)—is claimed to be 100 per cent, as strong as the untied line.

KNOT SECURITY

Knots which perform well when steadily loaded—strong knots—may slip, capsize or fall apart quickly when subjected to intermittent jerking: though they are strong, they are "insecure." *Strength and security are two different and quite separate considerations.*

A Double Sheet Bend (Fig. 14C-D) may be no stronger than the Common Sheet Bend (Fig. 14A), but it is definitely more secure and should be used when security is essential. (The Common Sheet Bend is about equal in strength to the so-called "left-handed" version of the knot, in which the short ends finish on opposite sides. The left-handed version, however, is significantly less *secure*, which is why the correct method of tying it is stressed, with both short ends on the same side.)

Selecting the best knot for the job is clearly a fine art, but it is *not* a precise science—not yet. We really know very little about what goes on inside a knot. Testing and measuring knot performance could be a fascinating pastime and a fruitful field of research. Where there is general agreement about a knot's breaking strength, that information is shown in brackets following the name of the knot.

ROPE STRENGTH

An extraordinary tug-of-war a couple of years ago ended in mishap when the 1½-inch-thick nylon rope snapped, injuring dozens of the 2,200 participants. And although the organizers of the event believed the rope was strong enough the wonder is that the rope withstood for 12 minutes the surging momentum of so many straining people.

Whether you need to moor a super-tanker to an oil rig or just fit a curtain pull to your venetian blind, you can get detailed performance specification for all ropemakers' products, including safe working loads. When in doubt, choose line with a much greater minimum breaking load than is strictly necessary. Lifeboat falls (the ropes which lower them into the water) are required to be six times stronger than what is actually needed to do the job.

Vegetable fiber ropes are weaker than man-made ones, and, strangely enough, new natural fiber ropes can be weaker than those made years ago. Vegetable fiber is only half as strong when wet; it has a low strength-to-weight ratio. Greater strength is obtained only by resorting to ropes of much larger circumferences (cables 24 inches in diameter were not unknown 200 years ago).

By comparison, strong man-made ropes are so light and thin that you may sometimes have to use an even stronger line than you need just to have something thick enough to grip comfortably. Synthetic line does not absorb water and the breaking strain remains constant when wet.

As mentioned previously, synthetic line has one major drawback; it deteriorates rapidly at high temperatures and melts at the following points: nylon—482°F (250°C); polyester—500°F (260°C); polypropylene—329°F (165°C).

Rope is expensive. Proper care will prolong its life and pre-serve its strength. Misuse, such as dragging it over sharp or rough edges or over surfaces where dirt and grit can penetrate between strands and yarns, will nick many of the individual fibers. The result will be a weaker rope, small sizes being more drastically affected than larger ones. Inspect your rope periodically and wash out dirt and grit. Avoid stepping on it or forcing it into harsh kinks. Rope that is slung over hooks to lift loads, or just tied around a car-towing eye, will be weakened by as much as 30 per cent.

Oddly enough, 4-strand rope is 11 per cent weaker than its 3-strand equivalent, and cable-laid line (3-strand ropes laid up left-handed to form a 9-strand cable) is 40 per cent weaker than the same size of hawser-laid (ordinary 3-strand) rope.

Old-time sailors referred to rope size by its circumference in inches. They estimated breaking strain by squaring the circum-ference and then dividing the product by any number from 2 to 12, depending upon the kind of rope and experience, to arrive at a breaking load in tons. You can still find these methods in print. Today, though, rope performance may be predicted with greater accuracy by using formulas and graphs. It's no longer sold by the fathom (6-foot lengths) but by the yard or the meter, and its size is the *diameter* measured in inches (roughly 25 mm).

UNTYING KNOTS

Generally knots should be untied after use, and this will be easier if you choose a suitable knot in the first place. Select a knot, if possible, which cannot jam and is easy to undo, such as the Lighterman's Back Mooring Hitch (Fig. 37), which will hold a tow of six loaded barges with a combined weight of hundreds of tons, but takes only seconds to cast loose in an emergency. The Timber Hitch (Fig. 18) is another such knot.

Use knots which disappear when slipped off their founda-tions, such as the Clove Hitch (Fig. 16), a Scaffold Hitch (Fig. 16C) and the Prusik Knot (Fig. 61).

Add a draw-loop. The knots will be no less strong or secure, but you can then undo them with a single tug. The Sheet Bend may be modified in this way (Fig. 14E), while the Highwayman's Hitch (Fig. 38) is nothing but a succession of draw-loops.

Find out which knots capsize into a different form and can then be slid apart, such as the Reef or Square Knot (Fig. 12), the Sheet Bend (Fig. 14) and the Bowline (Fig. 13).

Reduce knots to simpler forms: in the Fisherman's Knot (Fig. 15), for example, you can separate the two halves and untie each part on its own.

Don't break your fingernails. You can poke and pry stubborn knots apart with a spike.

Occasionally it may be necessary to cut line. *Never hesitate if it will prevent or reduce loss or harm to someone.*

UNTANGLING LINE

No matter how methodically you stow away line, when you go to use it again, it looks like a bird's nest. To sort out such a muddle, there is an effective trick. First, keep the tangle as loose as possible. Do *not* pull experimentally or impatiently so that the whole thing jams up. Locate the point where the end enters the tangle. Enlarge the opening around it, so that the tangle resembles a doughnut. Rotate this "ring" outwards so that the lengthening end of the rope continues to emerge from the center of the mess.

This method of untangling knots often works and is always worth a try. During my years as a swimming coach I always managed to untangle pool lane ropes this way, and they had floats attached every couple of yards. If the rope is too snarled up to use this method, there is no alternative but to go through the laborious process of pulling the loose end through again and again.

The Constrictor Knot

One knot has appeared in the last few years (its history is obscure) that is very special. It is the Constrictor Knot, which consists of a simple Overhand Knot trapped beneath a diagonal Round Turn (Fig. 6A) which acts just like a finger holding it secure. I cannot recommend it too highly. If you want a knot that will grip tightly and stay tied, learn this one.

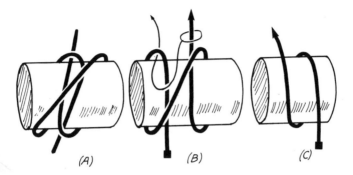

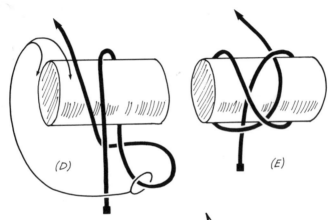

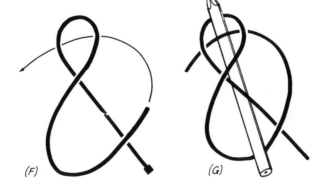

Fig. 6 Constrictor Knot

Use it as a temporary or semi-permanent whipping for the end of a rope. Use it instead of a vise or clamp to hold together items you've glued while they dry. Use it on the joints of pipes, in making kites and models, for rope ladders, to close the neck of a sack, etc. There's no end to its uses.

To tie the Constrictor Knot, make a Clove Hitch and then tuck the working end once more (Fig. 6B) to form the Overhand Knot beneath the Diagonal Round Turn. A really quick way—which can only be done near the end of the rope—is to take a Round Turn (Fig. 6C) and pull out a bight, which you then partially untwist (Fig. 6D) as you pass it over the end (Fig. 6E).

You can tie it in several other ways. Perhaps the best is one-handed: Make an ampersand (&) with the rope (Fig. 6F), passing the working end behind the upper loop. Pick up the resulting arrangement with a thumb and finger—or pass an object through it (Fig. 6G)—to transform it into the recognizable knot.

Important Tip

If the object you want to tie the knot around is soft and yielding (such as another rope), use hard cord which will bite into it.

If the object is hard (like a pipe or rail), use soft, stretchy material to tie the knot. The effect will be the same. In each case, it will grip like a boa constrictor. You can cut the ends off close to the knot for neatness with no risk of its coming apart.

You'll have to cut a Constrictor Knot off after using it. It's best to do this by slicing through the diagonal with a single cut. That way you protect whatever is beneath the knot from accidental damage, and the knot will fall into two halves.

ROPE ENDS

Whippings

Rope costs money. If it's cut, and the ends are left loose in any way, strands will unravel and the yarns fray until that portion of the rope can't be reconstructed. It's an expensive waste. Whipping prevents fraying and helps you to pass the ropes' ends easily through pulleys' eyes, and other tight places.

Three different methods will cope with all circumstances:
1. *The Constrictor Knot* (Fig. 6)—quick and effective;
2. *The Common Whipping* (Fig. 7A-C)—a neat and secure permanent treatment for rope ends that is easy to do and has been used for centuries;
3. *A Palm-and-Needle Whipping* (Fig. 8A-D)—an excellent whipping that should never come off, even though the rope's end is battered in a high wind. You can use it just as well on braided or sheath-and-core lines. After you apply wrapping turns, as you would for any whipping (Fig. 8A), create Riding Turns (diagonal turns that rest in each groove between the strands, (Fig. 8D). On an ordinary 3-strand rope use three riding turns. You make them simply by stitching the working end of the twine through each strand with a needle (Fig. 8B-D), snaking backward and forward from one end of the whipping to the other. Start at the outside end and, to finish off, stitch the end of your whipping twine back and forth across the body of the rope a couple of times.

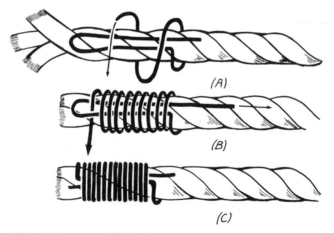

Fig. 7 Common Whipping

(A) *Make a bight in the standing end and wrap it tightly against the rope, as shown.*

(B) *Tuck the working end through the bight.*

(C) *Pull firmly on the standing end to trap the working end beneath the turns of the whipping. Trim both ends short.*

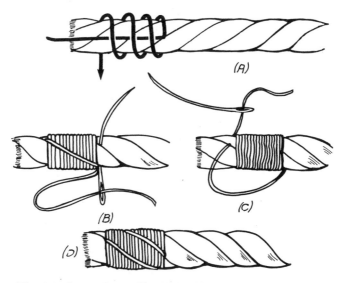

Fig. 8 Palm-and-Needle Whipping

Always bind *against* the lay of the strands, so that if there's any tendency for the line to open under a load, it will only tighten your whipping. Start the binding process away from the end of the rope and work towards it, trimming the end afterwards to within a quarter inch of the whipping. How near depends on the size of the rope. Whippings need to be as long as the width of the rope, or just a bit longer, and square. Use vegetable fiber twine on vegetable fiber ropes and synthetic thread on synthetic ropes.

Heat-Sealing Ends
When you apply a flame to synthetic yarns they melt and shrink away, leaving a small glob of molten material on the ends of the fibers. This quickly cools and congeals. *Sealing rope ends this way is lazy and dangerous.* A tugboat operator once sliced the palm of his hand open down to the sinews after the hardened (and obviously *sharp*) end of a rope that had been heat-sealed pulled through his grasp. There is no substitute for a properly made whipping.

Rope retailers measure out the line they sell and cut it by

means of an electrically heated "guillotine," which does a neat job without leaving the ugly, oversized glob of hardened plastic that can inflict wounds.

Other Methods with Ends

Some boat chandlers sell a special pair of pliers which apply expanded collars to rope ends. This ingenious device, together with a supply of the right size rubber collars, can be useful to anyone handling ropes. A roll of adhesive tape is almost as good. Neither, however, can replace the longer lasting, more attractive, traditional whipping.

Stopper Knots

A Stopper Knot stops the end of a rope, cord or smaller material from coming out of a hole. Needleworkers tie a Stopper Knot in thread when they sew, to prevent it from pulling through the material. Construction workers tie a Stopper Knot in the rope that passes through a pulley to stop it from unreeling. You can use a Stopper Knot to attach the string that turns on a light or to restring a musical instrument, or in hundreds of other ways.

All the Stopper Knots shown here build from a Simple Overhand or Thumb Knot (Fig. 9A), which is the simplest type.

The Figure of Eight Knot (Fig. 9B), so-called because of its outline, is also known as the Flemish Knot. Start it as if you're going to tie an Overhand Knot, but give the loop half a twist before you tuck the end through it.

The Stopper Knot (Fig. 9C) begins as a Figure of Eight Knot, but it gets an extra half twist before the end is tucked. The Stevedore Knot (Fig. 9D) is a Stopper Knot with an extra half twist before tucking.

> *Note:* All the Stopper Knots look different when they're pulled tight than they do in flattened-out diagrams. The pull is on the standing part only, dragging down the short end until it projects more or less at right angles to the line. The end is trapped within a top bight, while the body of the knot winds into a collar around the body of the rope, forming the stopper. Don't use Stopper Knots in place of whippings, except when you're working with very small twine.

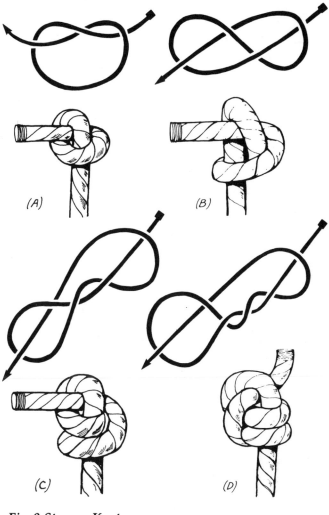

Fig. 9 Stopper Knots
(A) *Overhand Knot.*
(B) *Figure of Eight Knot.*
(C) *Stopper Knot.*
(D) *Stevedore Knot.*

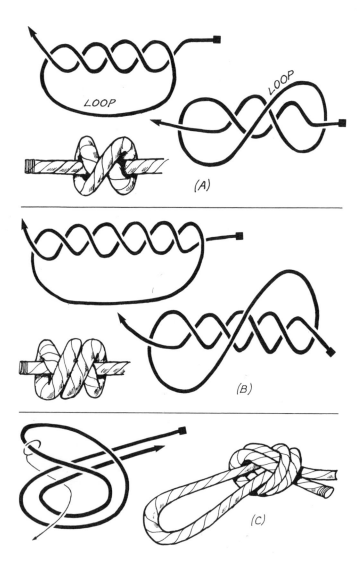

Fig. 10 Multiple Overhand (Blood) Knots
(A) Double Overhand Knot.
(B) Triple Overhand Knot.
(C) Overhand Loop Knot.

A Double Overhand Knot (Fig. 10A), an Overhand Knot enlarged by tucking the working end through its own loop two, three, four or more times, a Triple Overhand Knot (Fig. 10B) and all of these Multiple Overhand Knots are known as "Blood Knots." They may have gotten that name because surgeons used them to tie severed blood vessels, or it may be because they're found in the lashes of some whips.

There is a special technique for tying them. Do *not* pull on both ends of the line. Instead, keep the knot open and loose. Pull very gently on each end at the same time as you steadily twist the two ends of the line in opposite directions. You'll soon find out which way to twist. If you go the wrong way, nothing much will happen. If you go the right way, the knot will twist into shape, with the loop wrapping itself around in a spiral. Take the time to master this method. You'll find later that quite a few knots are tied the same way. Continue to work the knot tighter and snugger while permitting the knot to settle itself the way it wants to go.

The Overhand Loop Knot (Fig. 10C) is an Overhand Knot "tied in the bight." It makes a fairly clumsy Stopper Knot, but its extra bulk can prove invaluable when you want to string a musical instrument.

TIGHTENING KNOTS

Working with Stopper Knots points up the principles of tightening any knot:

1. It's important to know what the finished knot should look like.
2. Newly tied knots need to be "encouraged" in the direction of their finished form by patient pushing.
3. Tighten them by gradually removing slack from each part of the knot in turn, a little at a time.
4. Never distort the knot beyond recognition by just tugging on both ends. Very few knots can be tightened by pulling the two ends. Even the Reef (or Square) Knot (Fig. 12) has four parts emerging from the knot, and each should be pulled gently in turn to get the knot settled down evenly.
5. Knotted rope or cord knows which way it wants to lie. You can't force it to do differently. For example, the Figure of

Eight Knot (Fig. 9B) will always have its end askew. If it's important for the end to be fairly straight, pick another knot (say, the Double Overhand Knot, Fig. 10A).

KNOTS, BENDS AND HITCHES (DEFINITIONS)

A *knot* is a knot, strictly speaking, only when it is either tied in the end of a line as a stopper, forms a loop or noose or is made in two ends of the same piece of line (in tying up a package, for instance), as in the Constrictor Knot. The term "knot" is also used when two pieces of very small stuff are tied together (such as anglers' monofilaments).

A *bend* (such as the Full Carrick Bend, Fig. 29) joins two free lines together. So one rope is said to be "bent to" another. Bends generally unite ropes of *equal* thicknesses. Certain bends will cope with lines of very different sizes (the Sheet Bend, the Full Carrick Bend, the Bowline Bend and the Heaving Line Bend, for example), and where such bends appear in this book, that fact is either pointed out or is obvious from the illustration.

A *hitch* (such as the Round Turn & Two Half Hitches [Fig. 17]) fastens a line to a post, ring or spar—or to another rope which takes no part in the actual knotting. To hitch the working end of one line onto the standing part of another, when the two lines differ in size, always assume the thinner one forms the hitch around the thicker one. It's just about impossible to make a secure hitch with a thick cord around a thin one.

LAYING UP STRANDS BY HAND

Neglected rope—and you see it everywhere, unwhipped and unraveling—is an expensive waste. It shouldn't be allowed to get to that state. Before re-whipping it, try to avoid cutting off the unraveled section by laying up the strands again. It may be possible to put them back together, although extremely tight-laid line (done by machine, remember) can never be quite the same when re-laid by hand.

Use your knowledge of twist and countertwist to reproduce the lost section of rope. Spread and hold the three strands between the forefinger and thumb of one hand. Curl the remaining three fingers around the body of the rope itself. With your other hand give a strong left-handed twist (counter-clockwise as you look at the end of the strand) to the uppermost strand, so as to tighten its left-handed lay even more. Then immediately pull it over and down behind the other two strands, trapping it there.

What was the middle strand has now come out on top. Continue to twist and then re-lay each strand as it becomes the top one, drawing the completed rope half-an-inch at a time through your gripping hand with your spare fingers. Finally, whip your handiwork (Fig. 7).

Using this technique you can actually make up short lengths of your own cordage using any kind of small material, and any combination of colors. Taking thin and comparatively weak threads or cords, you can produce an original, thicker and stronger product.

SWIGGING (Fig. 11)

I learned this technique sailing whalers as a boy.

If the mains'l had even one small wrinkle in it, the grizzled old mariner would want the main halyard (rope) hauled down tighter. But it would be straining so much already that just pulling on it would gain nothing. In fact, once it was cast loose, it would snatch back and you'd lose more than you stood to gain.

"Swig up," he'd growl, and he'd be right. Do not let the line go completely from its belaying point (the cleat where it is made fast, for example). Leave at least a Half Turn (Fig. 11A) around some firm support. The friction will enable you to hang onto what you've got. Then, holding this Half Turn firm with one hand, grasp the standing part with the other and pull it out of line (Fig. 11B) like a bowstring. The leverage is so great you'll always be able to gain some slack this way.

The next stage is where you "win over" the rope—but you must be quick. Let the bent rope go with a twang, just as if you were releasing a bowstring (Fig. 11C), but at the same moment pull in on the other hand. You'll gain some extra inches of line which you can then hold via the friction of the half turn. Repeat the process rhythmically—heave in, release and pull—several times. It will be a fight and the rope will creak alarmingly, but that's the way to do it. Finally, tighten it firmly.

This is also a useful technique to tighten up loads on car luggage racks, for raising flags and even for tying packages.

Fig. 11 Swigging

FORMING LOOPS

This way of manipulating lines can make your knot-tying much more skillful. It can help you tie several knots, especially when the rope is already under a moderate amount of strain and there is little or no slack available in the standing part (such as in the Bowline (Fig. 13G-H) and the Sheepshank (Fig. 21E-F).

Make a Half Hitch (Fig. 13G). Now pull the working end of the line in the direction of the arrow until it springs straight. You'll find that the standing part now forms a loop around the working end instead. Pull that part straight, removing the loop, and it will reappear in the first part.

3 • BASIC KNOTS

Everyone whose work involves rope uses the same few basic knots. During my 10 years working on a commercial tideway, I saw mariners of all kinds, merchant seamen of many nations, river police, harbor masters and customs crews tying knots. They had all settled on the same ones, which they used for mooring ships, shifting heavy cargo and doing every possible job—from hanging out their washing to recovering decomposing corpses. The knots that were trusted by these hardy professionals clearly merit attention. There were seven:

Two knots—the Reef or Square Knot (Fig. 12) and the Bowline (Fig. 13);

Two bends—the Sheet Bend (Fig. 14) and the Fisherman's Knot (Fig. 15—yes, it is a bend, see page 52);

Three hitches—the Clove Hitch (Fig. 16), the Round Turn & Two Half Hitches (Fig. 17) and the Timber Hitch (Fig. 18).

These knots have certain good features in common. They're easy to learn and tie. Each one has a distinctive appearance, so you know when you've got it right. They are easy to untie and cast off, and you can retie them repeatedly without ruining the line. You can even tie them one-handed, and that can be vital. "Use one hand for the job—keep the other for yourself" means, in other words, "Hang on!" That advice is drilled into every young seaman, and is just as important for rock climbers, window cleaners or lumberjacks.

Reef (or Square) Knot (Breaking Strain 45%; Fig. 12)

The Reef Knot (often called the Square Knot) is flat, symmetrical (Fig. 12A) and made of two interlocked bights with both short ends on the same side.

If it isn't flat, it's a Granny Knot. If the ends are on opposite sides, it's a Tumbling Thief Knot (Fig. 86). Neither is as strong nor as secure as the Reef Knot.

Tie it by placing one Overhand Knot on top of another, taking care that one of the knots is left-handed and the other right-handed. Remember: "Tie left over right, then right over left" (Fig. 12B-D).

You can quickly free Reef Knots by pulling sharply on one end (Fig. 12E). This capsized version is a Lark's Head Knot (Fig. 12F), which you can slide apart fairly easily. Releasing the Reef Knot is easier still, if—as you tie it—you leave one end drawn only part of the way through to form a quick release draw-loop. This makes a Single Reef Bow.

When both ends form draw-loops (like tying shoelaces), it's a

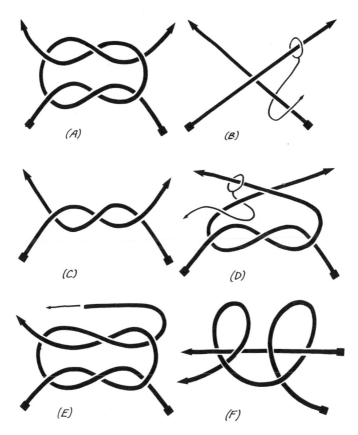

Fig. 12 Reef Knot

Double Reef Bow. That is, sad to say, the only knot most parents ever teach their children.

Incidentally, just as many people unknowingly tie a Granny Knot, many use a Double Granny Bow when tying their shoe laces. This will work loose much more often than a Double Reef Bow. So if you've just been accepting that it's routine to retie your shoe laces several times a day, you're probably not using the Double Reef Bow.

Never use a Reef Knot as a *bend*. It is strictly a *knot*, used for packages or binding by tying two ends of the same piece of line. This way the actual knot presses against whatever it is holding. It is ideal for bandages and slings—and for scarves, too. Don't use it to join pieces of rope or lines of different diameters. It could slip or jam, and either way it's unreliable.

The Reef Knot is ancient. Late Stone Age people knew the differences between a Reef Knot and a Granny Knot. Greeks and Romans called it the Hercules Knot. The ease with which it can be spilled to form a Lark's Head Knot, and then slipped apart, makes it perfect for reefing sails, which is how it got its name.

Bowline (Breaking Strain 60%; Fig. 13)

The Bowline (Fig. 13A) forms a loop that will not slip in a single end of line. The left-handed Bowline (Fig. 13B) is less secure, so don't use it.

To tie the Common Bowline, first form a loop in the standing part of the line, as shown in the illustration. Next, pass the working end up (Fig. 13C) through the eye of the loop, around the back of the standing part, and then back down through the eye once more. Practice it until you can tie it quickly with your eyes closed.

It's a simple, strong and secure knot, and the greater the strain placed upon it, the tighter it holds. You can always untie it easily by pushing forward the bight which encircles the standing part of the line. Use it for climbing, lifesaving and boating, and in the end of package string.

The Running Bowline (Fig. 13D) makes a noose which readily falls open once tension comes off it. The Bowline Bend (Fig. 13E) is used to join large, less manageable ropes or cables temporarily, just as illustrated, with two Common Bowlines interlocked. The ropes may be of different thicknesses.

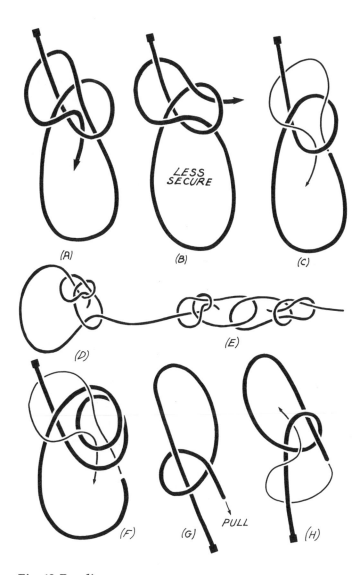

Fig. 13 Bowline
(G)-(H) *Tying a Bowline upside down by forming a loop in the working end and transferring it to the standing part.*

A word of caution: The Bowline may be a little less reliable in modern synthetic ropes, so secure the end with an extra Half Hitch or tuck it and trap it beneath one of the rope's strands. Use a more secure version—the Double Bowline (Fig. 13F)—if the knot is likely to be towed over rough ground or through water.

It takes practice learning to tie the knot when you're looking at it from the wrong direction! Therefore, spend time now learning to tie it "upside down" (Fig. 13G-H). Also see the section on "Forming Loops" on page 45.

Sheet Bend (Breaking Strain 50%; Fig. 14)

The Sheet Bend (Fig. 14A) has the same layout as a Bowline (Fig. 13), but it reacts differently to strain. It's used for joining two lines together. They may be of slightly different diameters, but too great a difference in thickness would make the bend insecure and should be avoided.

To tie the Sheet Bend, form a bight in one line (if the lines are of different thicknesses, form the bight in the thicker line). Pass the working end of the other (thinner) line up through the eye you've formed, around the back, and trap it in place under its own standing part (Fig. 14B). Make sure you don't go back down through the bight. Note that both short ends finish up on the same side.

If the bight is made in inflexible material, it has a tendency to open up. To counteract this, make a second turn around the neck of the bight with the working end. This results in a Double Sheet Bend (Fig. 14C-D). You can leave a draw-loop (Fig. 14E) as a quick-release device in either knot.

A good utility bend that can withstand a great deal of strain, the Sheet Bend is easy to undo afterwards, even without a draw-loop, by rolling forward the bight that encircles the single line. If you tie this knot with short ends on opposite sides, you've made a left-handed Sheet Bend, which is less secure and should be avoided.

You can adapt the principle of the Sheet Bend to tie a line to anything that has an opening through which a single line may be passed and trapped beneath itself—such as the handle of a spade or any tool that needs to be lifted or hung by a rope.

Though the Sheet Bend is pictured in Ancient Egyptian art, it first appeared in print under the name "Sheet Bend" in 1794 because it secured ropes (known in nautical circles as "sheets") to sails. Before that it had a number of other names, the most usual being the "Common Bend" (it's still called that in some books) and the "Swab Hitch" when it was used to attach rope handles to mops.

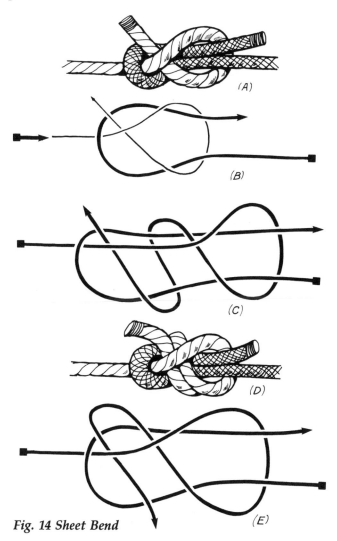

Fig. 14 Sheet Bend

Fisherman's Knot (Breaking Strain 65%; Fig. 15)

The Fisherman's Knot (Fig. 15A) is a compact arrangement of two Overhand Knots embedded, one against the other, with short ends on opposite sides, lying almost parallel to their nearest standing part. Tie it by positioning the two lines alongside one another facing opposite directions. Tie an Overhand Knot

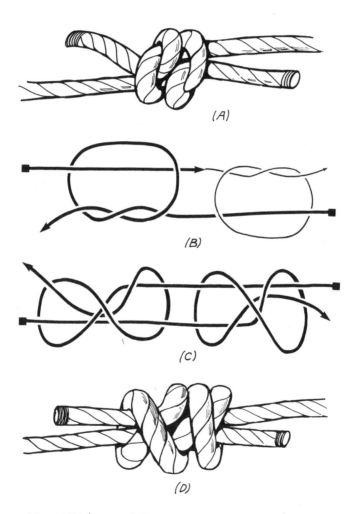

(A)

(B)

(C)

(D)

Fig. 15 Fisherman's Knot

with one end (Fig. 15B) so that you enclose and grip the standing part of the other line. Then reverse the lines and make an identical Overhand Knot with the other end, enclosing its nearby standing part. Pull the two knots together.

Use this knot to join lines of equal thickness. Climbers use it; so do anglers. You can tie it with small stuff or rope, but generally it's recommended for small cord and twines, since the sharp curves might be too harsh for big hawsers.

Tie a Double (Fig. 15C) or Triple Overhand Knot in each end and you have a Double (Fig. 15D) or a Triple Fisherman's Knot, which is supposed to be stronger. *Note:* Don't confuse this with the knot called the Fisherman's Bend (Fig. 17D)—which is a hitch.

The Fisherman's Knot is actually a *bend*, and it is relatively strong. Because it is tied in small stuff, it is called a "knot" (see the definition on page 42). Some writers strongly recommend it; others ignore it. Seamanship manuals omit it most of the time, perhaps because of the prejudice against using it in large sizes of rope. The only time I tied it in two hawsers, it jammed in so firmly that I had to cut it out with an axe! Yet, some authorities claim that it is easy to loosen, even in large rope. Normally, you can pull it apart and deal with the two Overhand Knots separately.

Known to the Ancient Greeks, this knot has picked up many names over the centuries. You can still find it mentioned in some books as the Englishman's Bend, the Halibut Knot, the True Lover's Knot or Bend, the Water Knot, the Waterman's Knot and the Angler's Knot.

Clove Hitch (Breaking Strain 75%; Fig. 16)

The front view of a Clove Hitch (Fig. 16A) resembles the letter "N" (the diagonal part may go either way, so sometimes the N is written backwards). The Clove Hitch is used to fasten a line to a rail, post or bollard, or onto another rope which is not part of the knot (but only if the strain will remain steady and at right angles). You can also use it to hang things in your garage, or scenery backstage, and it's often used to suspend a fender from a boat, though it's not a very secure mooring hitch. Distorted (Fig. 16B), it makes a safe Scaffold Hitch (Fig. 16C).

Tying the Clove Hitch is quick and easy, and there are many

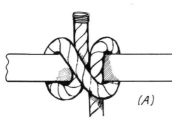

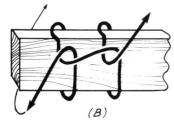

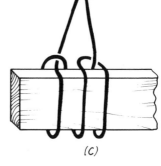

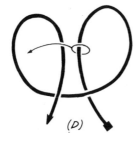

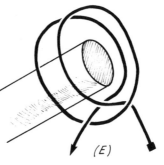

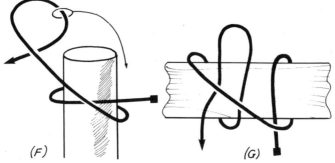

Fig. 16 Clove Hitch

different ways to do it. Basically, pass the working end around the rail or post; and cross the standing part at the front. Take another trip around in the same direction, then trap the end beneath the diagonal. If the end of the line is hard to reach or you simply want to make the knot more quickly, form two opposing loops (Fig. 16D) and cross them—placing the second one on top of the first—and slip the result over the post (Fig. 16E).

If you're working with a vertical post, apply an underhand loop (Fig. 16F) as a device to slow and stop the load on the line; then lock it in place with a second Half Hitch (Fig. 16G). It's best to form loops in large sizes of rope while it's lying on the ground or deck—either with one hand or with a longshoreman's hook—and then pick up the two parts together. If the cord is small, you can tie it with only one hand—with a little practice.

The Clove Hitch is one of the most valuable hitches, provided the strain always comes from the same direction. Otherwise, it quickly works loose. Slip it off the end of the spar around which it was tied and it just falls apart. If great strain is going to be applied to it, and the diameter is small, use a draw-loop (Fig. 16G).

The name Clove Hitch was first used in William Falconer's *Universal Dictionary of the Marine* in 1796. In 1884, the knotting authority Burgess wrote of the Clove Hitch: ". . . made in the bight as if it was a single piece of line, this tie is often used by surgeons in cases of dislocation of the thumb." (Ouch!)

Round Turn & Two Half Hitches (Breaking Strain 70%; Fig. 17)

The name describes exactly what this knot looks like: a Round Turn (Fig. 3) secured by two hitches, one beneath the other (Fig. 17A). Use it any time you need to attach a line securely to a beam, rail, pole, ring, hook or handle. It moors boats safely and will support loads of any description. It's a real all-around knot.

To tie it, take the working end around the pole to make a Round Turn (Fig. 17B), slowing and holding the load—whatever it is—by friction. Secure it with two Half Hitches (Fig. 17C), working them up snugly against each other and the first part of the knot. For extra security, especially if the line is likely to get wet or slippery, pass the first Half Hitch *through* the Round Turn.

This forms a Fisherman's Bend (Fig. 17D, breaking strain 75 per cent, which of course is not a bend at all, but a hitch). Don't be tempted to use the Fisherman's Bend instead of the Round Turn & Two Half Hitches for everything. If it has a load on it, you may be unable to free it when you need to.

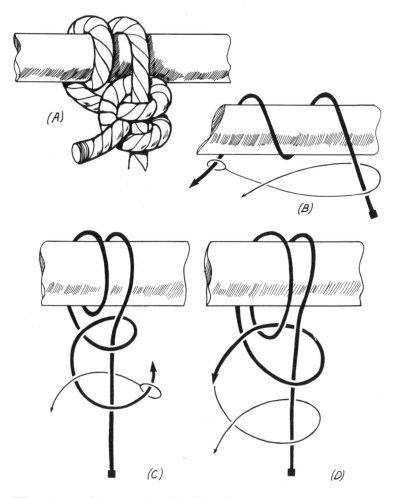

Fig. 17 Round Turn & Two Half Hitches
(A)-(C) Round Turn & Two Half Hitches.
(D) Fisherman's Bend.

The Round Turn & Two Half Hitches is one of the most commonly used hitches. It's strong and secure; it never jams; and it's good when tied over something of small diameter.

Timber Hitch (Breaking Strain 70%; Fig. 18A)

The Timber Hitch is a temporary noose made by doubling the working end back on itself and wrapping (or "dogging") it around its own standing part (Fig. 16B-C) several times. This only works if the noose remains firmly around some object. Often, there is a Half Hitch added some distance from the original knot, in which case the arrangement is called a "Killick Hitch" (Fig. 18D). The appearance of a Timber (or Killick) Hitch is unmistakable.

Use the Timber Hitch for towing, dragging, lifting or lowering logs, planks, poles, piling, scaffolding (or anything else that is long and relatively thin) through water, over land or in the air.

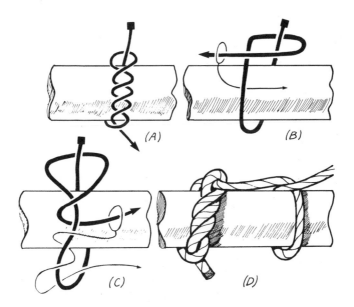

Fig. 18 Timber Hitch
(A)-(C) Timber Hitch.
(D) Killick Hitch.

4 ♦ STRING

"String
Is a very important thing,
Rope is thicker,
But string is quicker."
—*Spike Milligan*

String, twine, cotton, ribbon or thread—whether you use it for packages, needlework or in the garden—doesn't need expert knotting. It's too thin or crude for elaborate knots anyway. And, because it's fairly cheap, it doesn't matter if knots cannot be untied and have to be cut off after use. So you can use knots which may not generally be recommended for use with rope.

SIMPLE STRING KNOTS AND THEIR USES

The simple Overhand or Thumb Knot (Fig. 19A) may be used instead of whipping to stop twine fraying or cotton pulling through material. An Overhand Knot tied in the bight (Fig. 19B) forms a quick loop to attach by means of a "Bale Sling" Hitch (Fig. 39) to a ring or hook.

The simple Noose (Fig. 19C) is a start for tying packages (discussed in Chapter 8).

The Slip Knot (Fig. 19D) differs from a Noose by the position of its short end and its behavior. It can be just another stopper or the basis for a large number of useful Packer's or Package Knots. The Slip Knot (Fig. 19E), its short end stopped with an Overhand Knot, is another way to start tying packages. Another Packer's Knot (Fig. 19F) uses a Slip Knot but locks the end with a Half Hitch. Fig. 19G shows another variation of a Packer's Knot.

You can also tie the Overhand Knot in the ends of two parallel strands (Fig. 19H), as the needleworker does when using a doubled thread. Or you can create a Collection Knot (Fig. 19I), gathering together several strands to form a fringe or tassel. The Water Knot (Fig. 19J) is an Overhand Bend.

58

The Figure of Eight Knot (Fig. 19K) is a somewhat bulkier Stopper Knot than the Overhand Knot. The Figure of Eight Knot tied in the bight (Fig. 19L) forms a stronger loop, and is even bulkier. The Flemish Bend (Fig. 19M) is two lines joined by Figure of Eight Knots.

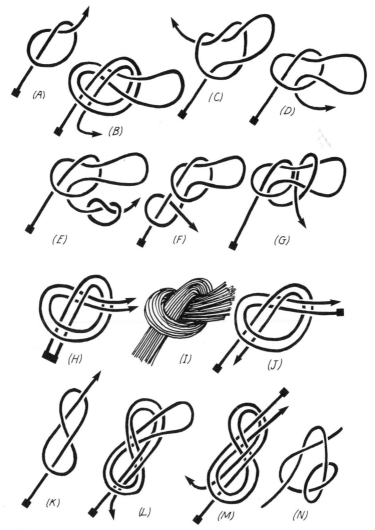

Fig. 19 String Knots

The Phoebe Knot (Fig. 19N), named after Clifford Ashley's daughter, is used to separate beads on a string. The Double Overhand Knot (Fig. 19O) can be either a Stopper Knot or another Bead Knot.

The Crossing Knot (Fig. 19P) is used to lock firm crossing points on parcels.

The Running Figure of Eight Knot (Fig. 19Q) is another effective packer's noose.

The Crabber's Eye Knot (Fig. 19R) is a Loop Knot which you may adjust for size and then lock by pulling one end.

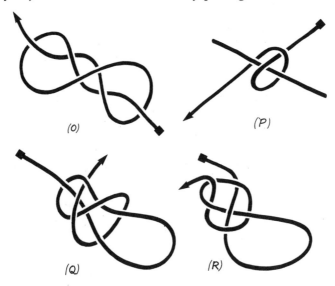

(O)　　*(P)*

(Q)　　*(R)*

Fig. 19 (continued) String Knots

KNOTS USED IN WEAVING (Fig. 20)

Weavers work with thinner, weaker threads and yarns. So they may use knots not generally recommended for use in rope (because they would jam, for instance); weavers can cut them off afterwards, or bury them from sight within their creations.

Knots are needed not only on warp (see Glossary) threads and weft wool but also as part of the primitive mechanism that operates the loom. Cords must be anchored to the loom's framework,

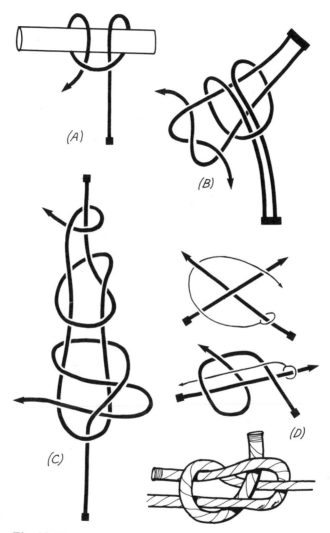

Fig. 20 Weaver's Knots

or passed through holes in it and secured with stopper knots. Treadles must be connected to harnesses or lams. Warp threads must be gathered together and fastened in bundles to apron sticks. Broken threads must be rejoined.

The following knots—some already discussed, others yet to
come—will also be useful to weavers and other craftworkers:
Reef Knot, Overhand Knot, Figure of Eight Knot, Clove Hitch,
Highwayman's Hitch, Ground Line Hitch and Round Turn &
Two Half Hitches (Figs. 12, 9A, 19K, 16, 38, 35 and 17, respec-
tively). In addition, there are a few knots peculiar to weaving:

Span Knot (Fig. 20A)

Tied with a long standing part and a short end, the Span Knot
is used to fasten any cord to the loom.

You can use it, for example, to attach a third harness at the
back; or to connect treadles to harnesses. The Span Knot is also a
way to temporarily fix a new length of warp thread to a pin in
the cloth, joining the two ends of a broken warp thread.

Snitch Knot (Fig. 20B and 20C)

The Snitch Knot is unique to weavers and essential for loom
adjustment. It's a nonslip but adjustable knot for attaching hed-
dles to pedals and lams so as to vary the height of the heddle
frames. I am assured by weaving friends that it is indispensable;
and they add that it's easier to support the weight of certain
loom parts during the tying process if the loop comes up from
below. To adjust, slide the loop upwards and tighten or loosen
the Half Reef Knot.

You can also improvise a Snitch Knot (Fig. 20C) with a single
cord. Tie the upper cord in a Loop Harness Knot, creating a
common Packer's Knot (Fig. 19F), while the lower cord makes a
Sheet Bend with draw-loop (Fig. 14E).

Weaver's Knot (Fig. 20D)

A great many knots are used to join a new piece of wool
(behind the heddle) onto the broken end; but the Sheet Bend
(Fig. 14), tied a special way, is the common Weaver's Knot. Always hold the end from the warp beam in the non-tying hand to
prevent the thread being pulled into the layers of warp beneath
it on the beam.

5 · MORE GENERAL KNOTS

Sheepshank (Fig. 21)

In 1627 the Sheepshank Knot was considered vital for all seamen. Strangely, it has become discredited. Some knot books now omit it. I see uses for it still.

It shortens a rope without cutting it (Fig. 21A), which saves money. It suspends slack lines out of harm's way (as you need to do with bell ropes). Modified, it is a Makeshift Purchase, the Waggoner's Hitch (Fig. 21B) used widely to tighten loads on trucks. *Note:* The twist in the long bight is a safeguard which prevents the knot spilling while it's being set up. A Sheepshank will also bridge a weak or damaged portion of a rope (Fig. 21C) that must be used regardless. This is perhaps its most useful— and least mentioned—function. Make sure that the damaged portion passes through both Half Hitches.

The Sheepshank has many advantages. It is tied in the bight of the rope—needing no ends—and is easy to learn. A quick alternative tying method is to make three loops (Fig. 21D), pulling the center one out through the other two. The knot holds under tension but falls apart when it goes slack. In fact, it is only secure under tension. You may also tie it by forming a loop in the bight (Fig. 21E) and transferring it with a tug to the single part of the line (Fig. 21F).

Transom Knot (Fig. 22)

The Transom Knot (Fig. 22A-B) is an excellent way to tie together cross-pieces of wood, bamboo and other materials (such as bean sticks and trellises in the garden). I also fix canoe paddles to my car luggage rack with Transom Knots. It's related to the Constrictor Knot, and—as with that knot—you can cut the ends short for neatness. Also, you can either cut the knot off by severing it on the diagonal so it falls away in two halves, or pry it apart with a pricker.

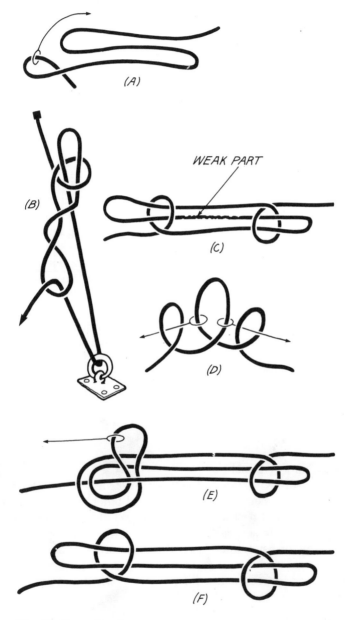

Fig. 21 Sheepshank

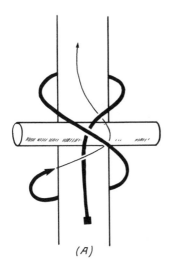

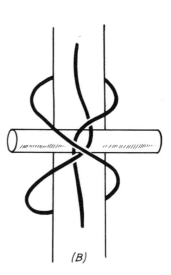

Fig. 22 Transom Knot

Strangle Knot (Fig. 23)

When used on just a single article, the self-same Transom Knot is a Strangle Knot (Fig. 23A-B), excellent for closing the neck of a sack, a roll of wallpaper or an inflated balloon. Tuck a draw-loop in a Strangle Knot (Fig. 23C) if you want the knot to be only temporary.

Cat's-Paw (Fig. 24)

Sailors and dock workers have been slinging heavy loads from crane hooks by means of this Strop Hitch and calling it by this name since at least the 1700s. *Note:* A strop is an endless sling which may be knotted—with a Double Fisherman's Knot (Fig. 15C-D)—but *should be spliced*. Simply hanging a single part of a loaded rope over a hook weakens it by about 30 per cent. The Cat's-Paw (Fig. 24A-C) drawn up snugly provides insurance: If one leg should break, the other may survive long enough to lower the load to the ground.

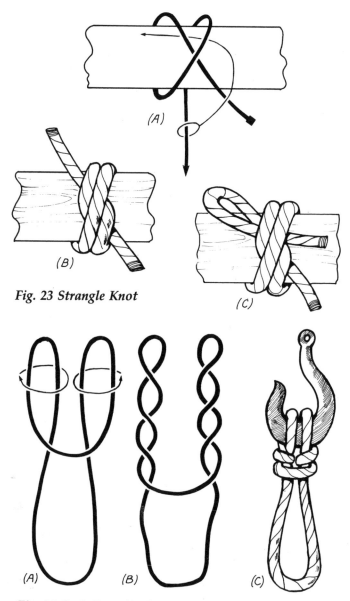

Fig. 23 Strangle Knot

Fig. 24 Cat's-Paw (Sailor's knot)

Hangman's (Jack Ketch's) Knot (Fig. 25)

This is a very strong noose designed to withstand heavy shocks. It does not always slide easily and is pre-adjusted to the required size. I was taught to tie it with seven turns (Fig. 25A-C). The way that Jack Ketch's Knot (Jack Ketch was a renowned hangman) is tied is a useful lesson. It's the basis for a Heaving Line Knot (Fig. 77) and, with a second layer of riding turns on top of the first seven turns, it's a useful way for scouts to carry emergency supplies of rope suspended by the loop from their belts.

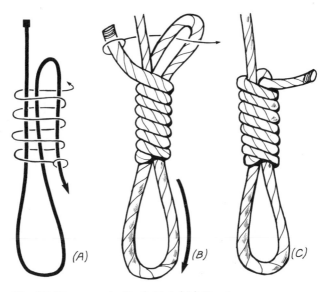

Fig. 25 Hangman's (Jack Ketch's) Knot

Jug (or Jar) Sling (Fig. 26)

A splendid knot designed to exert a tight grip around the smooth neck of a glass bottle or stone jar, the Jug Sling (Fig. 26) will carry containers of liquid safely (Fig. 26F) provided they have even the slightest raised lip. It is a useful knot to campers, picnickers and home wine makers. The large bight forms a natural handle and the two ends are knotted together (use a Fisherman's Knot) to form a second one.

Soft, stretchy material will grip better on hard, smooth sur-

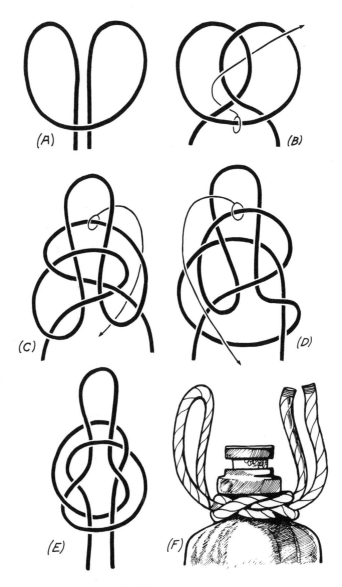

Fig. 26 Jug (or Jar) Sling
(C) *Pull rear bight down behind to create layout (D).*
(D) *Pull front bight down in front to create layout (E).*
(F) *Completed knot.*

faces. This secure and ingenious knot was used by the Romans. Cowboys found this knot made an effective hackamore or emergency bridle. The central crossed bights of the actual knot form a bit, the outer loops fitting around the animal's muzzle, while the long handles serve as the reins.

Decorative (Square) Knot (Fig. 27)

Do not confuse this knot with the Square Knot or Reef Knot (Fig. 12) on page 47.

This handsome, symmetrical knot makes an excellent tie for a scarf worn with an open-necked shirt or blouse. You can quickly become adept at tying and adjusting it beneath your chin with (or even without) a mirror. It also can be used to tie the sash on a dressing gown, when the ends hang down at just the right angle.

Figure of Eight Bend (Fig. 28)

The Figure of Eight Bend is a neat, strong bend (some say it's one of the strongest) in rope as well as short lengths of string. As the Figure of Eight Knot (Fig. 19K) is still known around the world as a "Flemish Knot," it's also called a "Flemish Bend." To tie it in rope, make a Figure of Eight Knot in one end, and then follow it around with the other working end.

Full Carrick Bend (Fig. 29)

This is a strong and secure working bend for joining large ropes and cables. The short ends (Fig. 29A-B) should be on opposite sides. Note how it capsizes, when drawn up, into an entirely different configuration (Fig. 29C). Don't worry. That's what should happen, so let it. The bend will even work in lines of different thicknesses—but not too different.

Even when the Full Carrick Bend is soaked it doesn't jam, which makes it ideal for towing lines and anchor cables; and it can be opened with a few light taps from the fat end of a fid. I've heard it recommended for climbers, although the ends project at awkward angles and it may prove too bulky to pass through a carabiner. Tied in small cord with both ends on the same side of the knot (Fig. 29D), it has a distinctive appearance which makes it popular with illustrators and designers, and it's also fine for scarves and sashes.

The name of the knot may have originated with a medieval type of Western European ship, the carrack. Carrick Roads, in England, is certainly a location where large numbers of these vessels prepared to sail and trade in convoy. But there could also be an Irish connection. Furthermore, this knot used to be called the Wake Knot since it was the heraldic badge of Hereward the Wake, a Saxon leader who refused to yield to William the Conqueror.

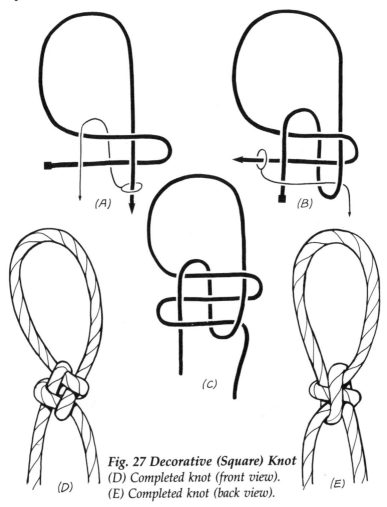

Fig. 27 Decorative (Square) Knot
(D) *Completed knot (front view).*
(E) *Completed knot (back view).*

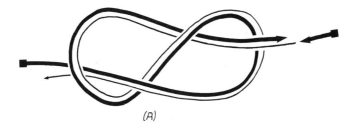

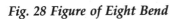

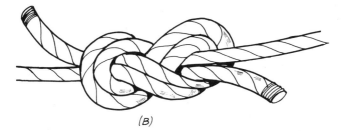

Fig. 28 Figure of Eight Bend

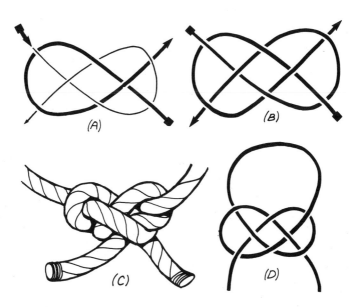

Fig. 29 Full Carrick Bend

Surgeon's Knot (Fig. 30)

Used by surgeons to tie off blood vessels, the Surgeon's Knot gets little attention outside that profession. But it's a good knot (Fig. 30A-B). See how it twists (Fig. 30C) as it's drawn tight, wrapping a diagonal around the top of itself. This must happen if the knot is to be fully secure.

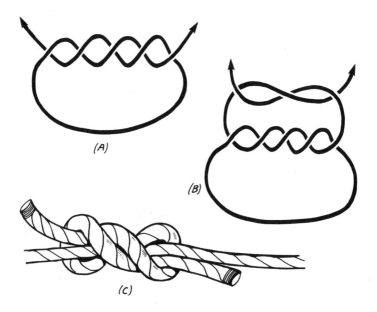

(A)

(B)

(C)

Fig. 30 Surgeon's Knot

True Lover's Knot (Fig. 31)

The basic True Lover's Knot (Fig. 31A-B) is of little practical use. As a loop knot in very small cord you can use it to form a string tie around your neck that will hold a whistle or stopwatch, a locket or an amulet of any kind (see Fig. 82, the Rope Ladder). A number of knots, including the Fisherman's Knot (Fig. 15), have been called True Lover's Knots. It's a name which seems to have appeared first in 1664, and it generally includes two Overhand Knots which are interlocked or intertwined to make a pleasing layout. This knot is the start of a very good fancy knot, the Shamrock Knot (Fig. 32).

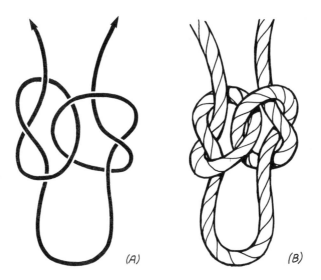

Fig. 31 True Lover's Knot

Shamrock Knot (Fig. 32)

This attractive, clover leaf knot (Fig. 32A-B) has been used by more than one knot-book illustrator as an eye-catching cover or title page decoration. It's also nice in ribbon on a gift-wrapped parcel; you can also tie it permanently in gold or silver wire to make original jewelry. It looks complicated, but it's only a True Lover's Knot with twin bights pulled out at the sides. Coax it into shape and pull it up tight with care and patience.

Rolling (Magner's, or Magnus) Hitch (Fig. 33)

The Rolling Hitch (Fig. 33A-C) is obviously related to the Clove Hitch, but is designed to take the strain of a lengthwise pull. Sailors, this is a hitch to secure a kicking strap on your dinghy. It is often used to secure a smaller line to a thicker rope, when it should be tied against the lay of the rope it's tied around. Note that there are two parts of the knot on the side from which the strain will come (Fig. 33C), so you must work out how to tie it either way.

Flag halyards are made fast to burgee staffs with a Rolling Hitch. It can be used to hoist aloft light tools, pipes and other long objects, or as a temporary mooring hitch for small craft on a tideway, where it is more secure than a Clove Hitch (Fig. 16). The name Rolling Hitch dates back to 1841. Before that it was referred to as Magnus Hitch or Magner's Hitch, a label which still causes confusion today. For a really heavy or fluctuating pull I prefer to use the Net Line Knot (Fig. 36).

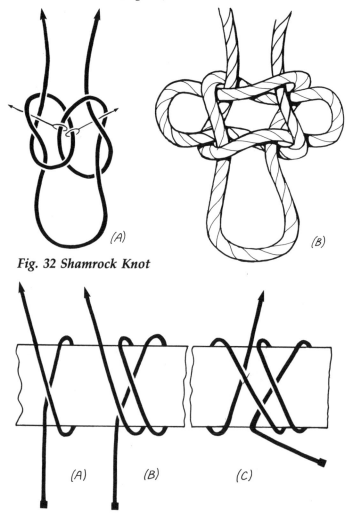

(A)

(B)

Fig. 32 Shamrock Knot

(A)　　*(B)*　　*(C)*

Fig. 33 Rolling (Magner's, or Magnus) Hitch

Buntline Hitch (Fig. 34)

Buntlines were ropes secured by this hitch to eyes on sails of square-riggers as an aid to furling them. They had to be secure against shaking adrift as they flogged about in the strong winds, so the short end is deliberately trapped inside the Buntline Hitch (Fig. 34A). This way it tends to jam, but that is its strength. It is the reverse of two natural Half Hitches, a good Packer's Knot for packages that want to unfold while you're tying them. Anglers may use it to fasten line to hook or swivel. Don't use it on lifelines or climbing ropes because of its reluctance to come apart, even when it's being untied, due to that short end trapped inside the loop.

Make the Buntline Hitch in flat material (Fig. 34B-C) and you have the knot often found in a man's necktie.

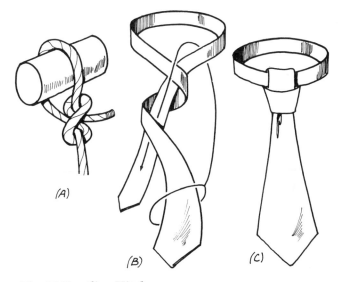

(A)   *(B)*   *(C)*

Fig. 34 Buntline Hitch

Ground Line Hitch (Fig. 35)

This little-written-about hitch was once used extensively by deep sea fishermen to attach drift-nets to the towrope, so it's a tough little knot. It was also used to tether cavalry horses to a picket rope. Today's horse riders might like to learn it. I use it in the end of a coil of line to keep it all together.

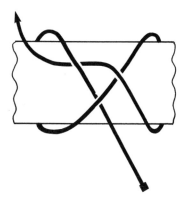

Fig. 35 Ground Line Hitch

Net Line Knot (Fig. 36)

Another fisherman's knot, the Net Line Knot has the advantage that it takes an extra turn around the foundation spar or rope, making it secure against a lengthwise pull in either direction. When I was a frogman working in London's canals and gravel pits, I learned to fasten my lifeline to my aqualung harness with a short lanyard and the Net Line Knot.

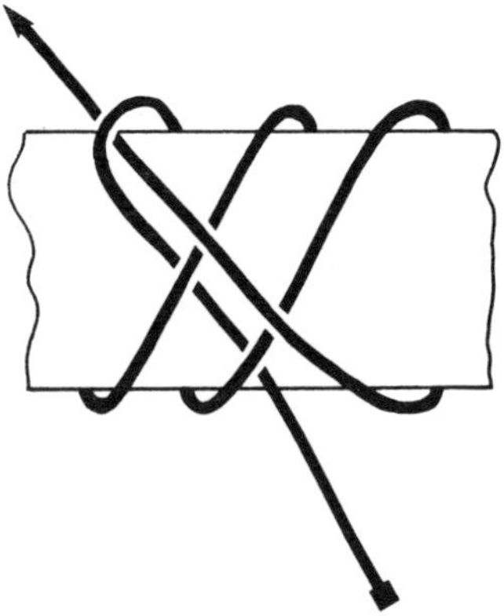

Fig. 36 Net Line Knot

Lighterman's Back Mooring Hitch (Fig. 37)

Taking in tow a drifting Thames barge was exciting and challenging work which I always enjoyed. Having one of those monsters—laden weight maybe a couple of hundred tons—

wallowing only feet from the stern of your boat, hung on the end of a towline 1½ inches in diameter which could part with the strain at any moment, made you choose with care the hitch you put around the oaken towing post midships. We always used the Lighterman's Back Mooring Hitch.

First, you take a Round Turn (or two, if you're unlikely to be able to hold the load otherwise—Fig. 37A); then hang on to the line while the coxswain eases the engine ahead and takes up the slack. Once the tow is set up as you want it, take a bight under and around the taut towrope (Fig. 37B) and hitch it over the top of the towing post (Fig. 37C). Finally, take the working end around the post once or twice so that it hangs there of its own weight.

This enormously strong hitch will hold anything, yet it can be cast free in a few life-saving seconds if things look as if they're going wrong. It is, of course, also first-rate for erecting marquees at fairs and bazaars. It is excellent for mooring craft, but then make sure the final turns cannot unwrap by attaching the loose hanging end to a convenient cleat.

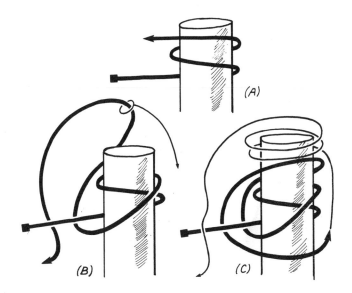

Fig. 37 Lighterman's Back Mooring Hitch

Highwayman's Hitch (Fig. 38)

The Highwayman's Hitch (Fig. 38A-C) is a slippery hitch, supposedly used by escaping robbers as a rapid release for their horses' reins. It is not featured in nautical manuals. I use it to hold objects temporarily when I need a third hand for craft or other do-it-yourself projects (I release it by pulling the end with my teeth); and it would be okay to moor a dinghy during a picnic, leaving a long enough end to be brought back aboard to cast off without stepping ashore again. Also, horseback riders and dog owners alike can safely tether their animals with this hitch. You might even train them to free themselves!

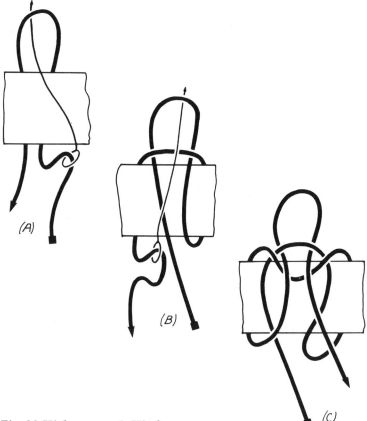

(A)

(B)

(C)

Fig. 38 Highwayman's Hitch

Bale Sling Hitch (Fig. 39)

This straightforward way to sling a load from a crane hook with a strop was in great use when sailing ships stocked up for months at sea with everything from live pigs to cannon barrels. At the upper end of the strop would be a Cat's-Paw Knot (Fig. 24).

Fig. 39 Bale Sling Hitch

Barrel Sling (Fig. 40)

How do you sling open containers that are still partly full? The answer is the Barrel Sling. A divided Overhand Knot (Fig. 40A) forms two elbow-like Single Hitches (Fig. 40B), one on either side of the load. Notice how the upper parts of rope leading to the lifting hook emerge outside the elbow crossings of the Single Hitches. There is no friction to keep them in contact with the load they surround once the weight comes off the sling, and the sling will fall away of its own accord. This is useful if you intend to remove it anyway.

When you plan to lift and deposit the load several times with the same sling, a slightly different layout—similar to a Figure of Eight Knot—is needed (Fig. 40C), and Marline Hitches (Fig. 40D) are formed. At first glance they are identical to Single Hitches, but they work differently. The upper parts of the rope appear from beneath the elbows and tend to cling to the sides of the load, even when there is no longer a strain upon them. This keeps the sling in position ready for the next time it's lifted, and can be a great saving in time and effort, if you're involved in a lot of cargo handling.

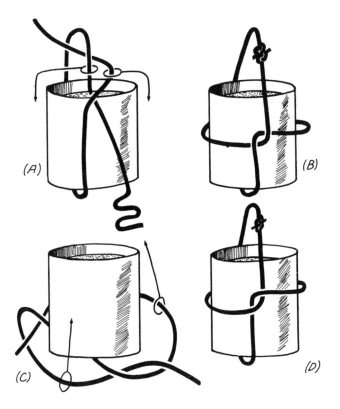

Fig. 40 Barrel Sling
(A)-(B) *Overhand Knot forms Single Hitches that fall away*
        when sling is unhooked.
(C)-(D) *Overhand Knot laid down like a Figure of Eight Knot forms*
        Marline Hitches, which tend to remain in place when sling
        is unhooked.

6 ◆ ANGLERS' KNOTS

Anglers are concerned about preserving the strength of their lines. They use specialized knots, bulky but streamlined, with many wrapping turns. How many turns, you will learn from experiment and experience. Some say five turns; others make as many as ten. Tying anglers' knots successfully in nylon mono-filament requires practiced fingers, lots of saliva (to lubricate the turns of the knots), pliers to pull them tight and nail clippers to snip ends close and neat.

The terms "bends" and "hitches" don't feature in anglers' ter-minology. There are just knots: My definition of a knot earlier includes *anything* tied in small material. Many traditional an-gling knots are no longer secured in modern nylon lines. Begin-ners might prefer to learn their knots in small cordage in home comfort before venturing to cope tying them in monofilament in the wet and freezing cold, at dawn beside the water. I am no angler, but the knots interest me. I can picture them and briefly describe their uses, but you need to ask another angler how to incorporate them into a tackle system.

Some years ago, a colleague at work asked me to make him a knotted net. Well, somehow I never got around to it—and now I'm glad I didn't. It's been explained to me that knotted mesh nets damage a fish's scales and fins and should never be used. Professionally made, knotless nets are better.

Bimini Twist (Breaking Strain 100%; Fig. 41)

This most remarkable newcomer, whether tied in monofila-ment or braided line, is claimed to be 100 per cent efficient (as strong as the unknotted line). Tied in the end of the reel line, it becomes the starting point for your tackle arrangement.

Make a large bight, a yard or so long, and wrap about 20 tight twists (Fig. 41A) into it. Transfer the bight from your hand by inserting both feet or knees into it so that you can steadily force it open sideways. This causes the inset turns to untwist (Fig. 41B-C) from the bottom upwards, at the same time winding on the working end from the top downwards to make a second layer of riding turns. Finish off with a couple of Half Hitches, the first around one part of the bight, the second around both parts (Fig. 41D).

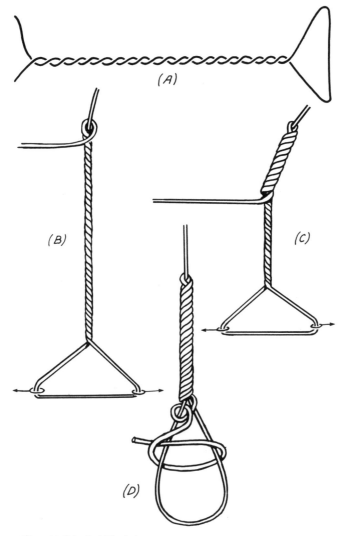

Fig. 41 Bimini Twist

Blood Bight (Breaking Strain 80%; Fig. 42)

This anglers' Loop Knot (Fig. 42A-B) appeared around 1947, if fishermen's tales can be believed. A stronger Loop Knot, it is, in fact, simply a Stopper Knot (Fig. 9C) tied in the bight.

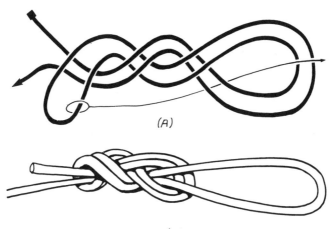

(A)

(B)

Fig. 42 Blood Bight

Loop Interlocked with Loop (Fig. 43)

This is a strong yet simple way to join a hook length of nylon to a reel line (Fig. 43A-B). It should look like a Reef Knot (Fig. 12). Don't let it get into a Lark's Head Knot (Fig. 43C) configuration, which is weaker.

Blood Knots (Breaking Strain 80%; Fig. 44)

Blood Knots join two lines together, generally of equal thickness.

Outward Coil (Fig. 44A-D): Bearing in mind that these knots draw up snug and small, never again to be untied, tackle-makers in the last century were able to keep how they were tied a trade secret. They'd make you as many as you wanted anytime, but you had to pay them. That is, until Jock Purvis, an engineer, ingeniously analyzed and reconstructed a specimen knot. He passed along his discovery to an angling author, who told the world in a 1910 publication. To tighten these knots, use the same technique as for Multiple Overhand Knots (page 41).

Inward Coil (Fig. 44E): More difficult to tie, this knot has a neater finish.

Improved Blood Knot (Breaking Strain 90/100%; Fig. 45)

To join two lines of different sizes, double the thinner line and wrap it a couple of turns more than the thicker line.

Perfection Loop (Fig. 46)

A popular old anglers' loop from about 1870, this knot survived the change from gut, and is just as effective in nylon. You can tie it quickly and easily with practice (Fig. 46A-B), but it is unsuitable for rope because it jams. One disadvantage might be the end which protrudes at right angles to disturb the water.

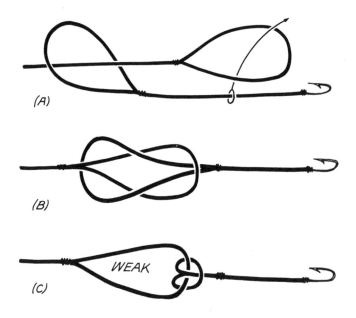

Fig. 43 Loop Interlocked with Loop
(A)-(B) Correct, strong.
(C) Wrong, weak.

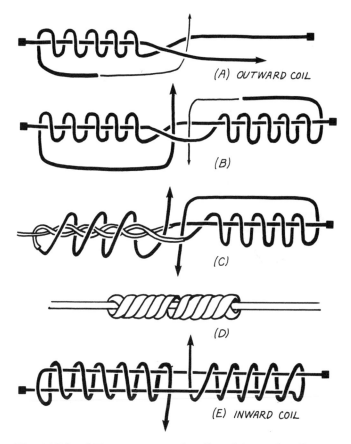

Fig. 44 Blood Knots: outward coil and inward coil
Note: All Blood Knots are tightened so that additional
contrary-twisting Riding Turns form as the bight (C) wraps
itself around the existing twists. These twists unwind a
corresponding amount, and the Riding Turns form.

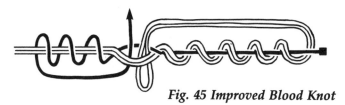

Fig. 45 Improved Blood Knot

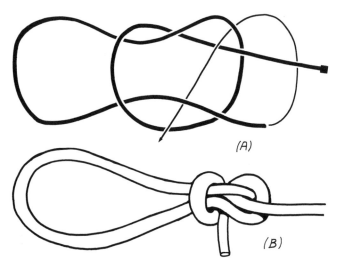

Fig. 46 Perfection Loop

Water Knot (Breaking Strain 95%; Fig. 47)

The earliest printed reference to this knot (Fig. 47A) is believed to be 1496—just 4 years after Columbus discovered America. It attaches a leader to the reel line, even if the sizes of the lines are different. To achieve the great breaking strain claimed for it, tuck the ends three additional times to create a Quadruple Overhand Knot (Fig. 47B) with both lines and draw them up as you would any Multiple Overhand Knot.

Loops to Line (Fig. 48)

You can use a modified Sheet Bend (Fig. 48A) to attach a fly line to a leader so that the end does not project at right angles, creating unwanted vibrations in the stream. For greatly different sizes of line, use an alternative method (Fig. 48B).

Quadruple Fisherman's Knot (Fig. 49)

It will be easier to tie this strong, barrel-shaped knot, with ends snipped off short, if you master the Fisherman's Knot (Fig. 15A-B) and the Double Fisherman's Knot (Fig. 15C-D) first.

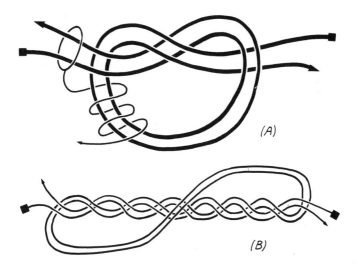

Fig. 47 Water Knot

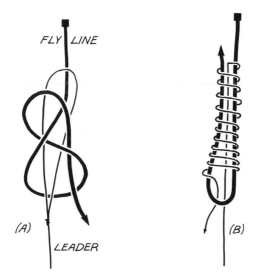

Fig. 48 Loops to Line

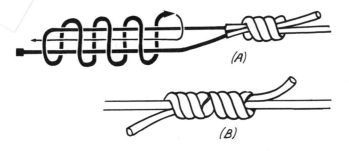

Fig. 49 Quadruple Fisherman's Knot

Overhand Loop (Breaking Strain 95/100%; Fig. 50)

This simple way to attach hooks, swivels, and so on, has become more widely accepted than more traditional knots.

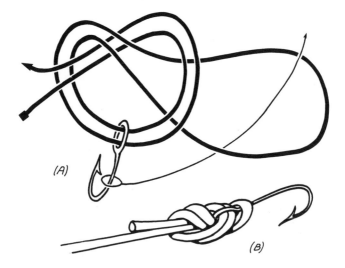

Fig. 50 Overhand Loop

Improved (Tucked) Half Blood Knot (Breaking Strain 95%; Fig. 51)

Make five turns—and double very thin line—to tie this knot.

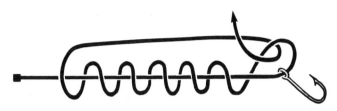

Fig. 51 Improved (Tucked) Half Blood Knot

Half Blood Knot (3½ turns) (Breaking Strain 80%; Fig. 52)

An old, still useful way to attach thicker lines to an eyed hook, this knot is recommended when the five turns of the Improved (Tucked) Half Blood Knot (Fig. 51) will not tighten snugly.

Fig. 52 Half Blood Knot (3½ turns)

Hook Tie (Breaking Strain 95%; Fig. 53)

Another strong attachment to an eye hook.

Fig. 53 Hook Tie

Double Stevedore Knot (Fig. 54)

For gut or nylon, this knot has the advantage of using a double thickness around the swivel ring.

Cat's-Paw for Anglers (Breaking Strain 95/100%; Fig. 55)

Anglers tie this knot differently from sailors or dock workers, rotating the swivel, etc., until they accumulate a sufficient number of turns.

Fig. 54 Double Stevedore Knot

Fig. 55 Cat's-Paw (for Anglers)

Turle Knot (Fig. 56)

Turle knots create a straight pull on any hook with a turned-down eye, such as fly-tied hooks. They were named after a Major Turle in 1884. First pass the line through the hook's eye, then form the knot and bring the hook up through it. Draw the knot snug on the upper side of the neck of the hook, making sure that the loop passes freely over the hackles of the fly.

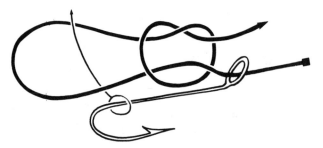

Fig. 56 Turle Knot

Double Turle Knot (Fig. 57)

This is a stronger version of the Turle Knot.

Fig. 57 Double Turle Knot

Improved Turle Knot (Breaking Strain 75/85%; Fig. 58)

Not quite as strong as the original Turle Knot, this version is considered more secure in nylon lines.

Fig. 58 Improved Turle Knot

Blood Dropper Loop (Fig. 59)

One of the best and strongest ways to create a paternoster system is to tie a Triple Overhand Knot (Fig. 59A) and pull down a bight (Fig. 59B). This gives you the required loop at right angles to the knot. (Paternoster line is fishing tackle in which short lines and hooks are attached at intervals to the main line.)

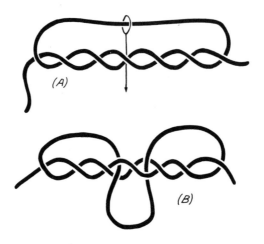

Fig. 59 Blood Dropper Loop

Whip Knot (Fig. 60)

This knot exerts a friction grip attaching a leader to a fly line (Fig. 60A), and should be reinforced by a suitable adhesive. You may want to adapt it to use as a secure knot for eyed hooks by reeving the end of the line through the eye first before tying; but it will also work on spade-ended (blind) hooks (Fig. 60B). It is easiest to make if you use a short separate length of nylon. Pass the end through the turns, and then tighten it with a wire loop needle (it is sometimes called a Needle Knot) or the hollow tube of an old ballpoint pen.

The cleverest way to tie it, once you have clearly in mind what the whipping should look like, is to wrap the turns from a large bight you deliberately form for that purpose (Fig. 60C). This will put a lot of twist into the standing part that you'll have to remove, or tightening the knot will be impossible. When you've seen it happen once or twice, you'll learn how to give the standing part just the right amount of twist in the other direction (in this instance counter-clockwise) before tying the knot. Then, as you wrap the required number of turns, undo the twist a corresponding amount. When no tension remains (Fig. 60D), the knot is ready for tightening.

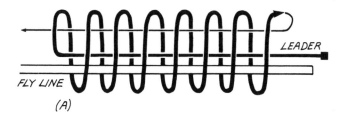

(A)

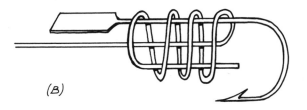

(B)

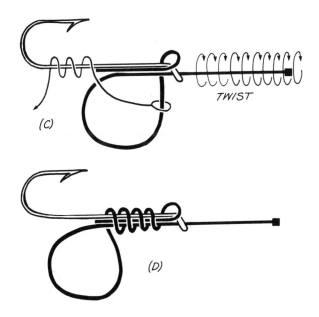

Fig. 60 Whip Knot

7 · CLIMBERS' KNOTS

Caution: I'm *not* a climber, but simply a student of knots. I can picture and describe them so that beginners are able to learn them in comfort and safety on the ground. It is important, however, that you seek the guidance of qualified instructors in order to determine how to make the knots work when you're actually climbing.

Also be sure to read the warning about man-made ropes in Chapter 1 (pages 22 and 23). *Man-made ropes melt with friction-generated heat, and thus part without warning, especially nylon climbing ropes. The result could be fatal.*

Prusik Knot (Fig. 61)

Named for Dr. Carl Prusik, who invented it in 1931, this climbers' device is designed to attach slings to ropes in such a way that they slide when the knot is loose, but seize and hold solid under a sideways load. It is used as a safety mechanism when abseiling or rappelling (see Glossary) down rock faces. It is also employed with two stirrups for climbing upwards. Rock climbers, spelunkers, tree surgeons, steeplejacks and others engaged in scaling tricky heights all need to know one or more Prusik-type knots.

Prusik knots grip and release with varying reliability and ease, but not one can be released easily while jammed and fully loaded. Weight must be taken off the knot, and the turns of the knot must then be manipulated to free them; sometimes you need to use both hands to do that, and many accidents—even death—have been the result.

Prusik knots (Fig. 61A-B) are usually based upon the Lark's Head Knot or Bale Sling Hitch layouts. For extra security in slippery conditions, use six coils (Fig. 61C). It is thought that a right-handed knot may hold better on right-handed rope; so use the left-handed version (Fig. 61D) on left-handed rope. On braided line, either will do.

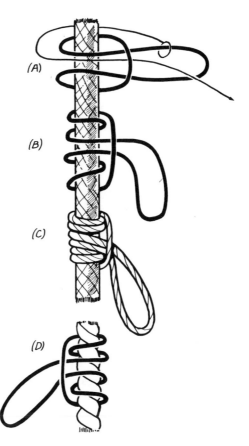

Fig. 61 Prusik Knot
(C) A 6-coil Prusik Knot gives a better grip.
(D) A left-hand Prusik Knot is used on left-handed line.

Munter Friction Hitch (Fig. 62)

This hitch (Fig. 62A), named after the man who introduced it in Italy in 1974 at the meeting of the Union Internationale des Associations d/Alpinisme, is the U.I.A.A. method of belaying (see Glossary), and widely accepted by mountaineers. Other names for it include Sliding Ring Hitch and Italian Hitch. The climbing rope is passed around and through the carabiner (a kind of snap-link) so that it will catch a falling climber by locking up. It can also be paid out or pulled in to give slack or tension as needed. It can be used for abseiling, but the practice is hard on the rope. (This dynamic hitch is based on the static Crossing Knot [Fig. 62B] still used today to stake out paths and erect barrier ropes at fairs and road work.)

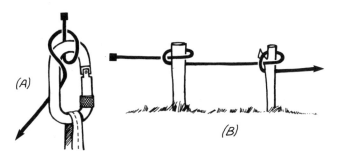

Fig. 62 Munter Friction Hitch

Double Munter Friction Hitch (Fig. 63)

The single version (Fig. 62) works fine with standard .44-inch (11-mm) rope, but smaller diameter rope such as .36-inch (9-mm) often needs more friction; this heavy duty version (Fig. 63A) provides it. The hitch may be tied in reverse (Fig. 63B-C).

Penberthy Knot (Caver's Helical Knot) (Fig. 64)

This knot and its variations are more reliable than the Prusik Knot and cannot truly jam; but they won't release easily when loaded. Cavers are said to find them effective.

There are three basic versions (Fig. 64A-C) with closures which have been described as either Sheet Bends or distorted Bowlines. It is a very open knot, and both the number of turns (from four to nine) and the amount of slack must be adjusted—with experience—to the weight of the person, the rope diameters involved and the material used. Too much slack and it slips; too little and it's hard to move. Opinions are divided whether the turns should be wound upwards or downwards but, if laid rope is used, there's an advantage from winding *with* the lay.

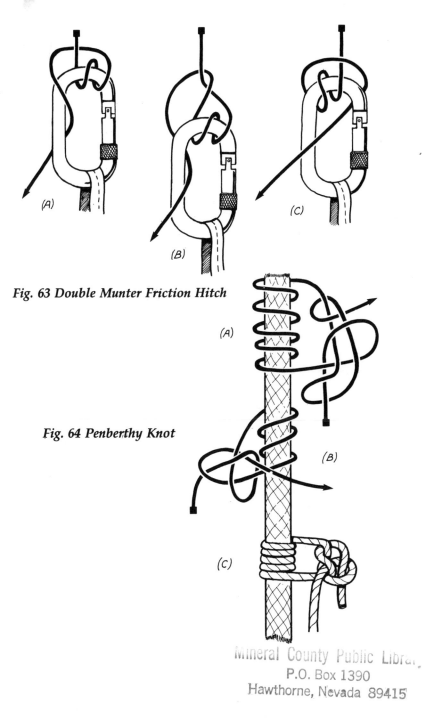

Fig. 63 Double Munter Friction Hitch

Fig. 64 Penberthy Knot

Hedden Knot (Cross Prusik Knot) (Fig. 65A)

Said to be about as good as the Prusik, it's harder to loosen. The Double Hedden Knot (Fig. 65B) gives more friction. It has a

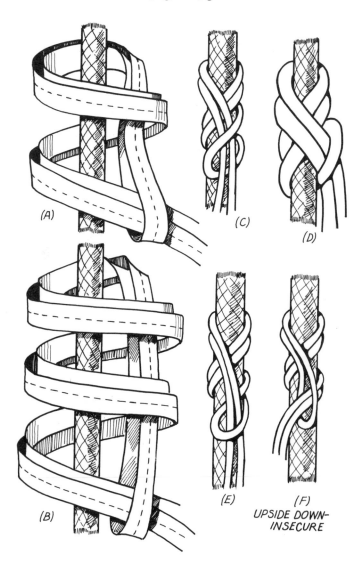

Fig. 65 Hedden Knot

slightly different appearance, even when tied identically (Fig. 65C-E) in slings of different sizes or with a twist. If tied upside down (Fig. 65F) it will slip, as the knot is directional in its ability to hold.

Tarbuck Knot (Fig. 66)

The Tarbuck Knot became obsolete with the advent of Kern-mantel (sheath-and-core) double braid ropes. These new lines absorb shock elastically and the sheath of a Kernmantel rope would be stripped by the slide-and-grip action of the Tarbuck Knot. So new knots have been developed and the Tarbuck Knot is rarely mentioned in modern climbing texts.

Though the Figure of Eight Loop (Fig. 70) is now used more than any other as the standard tie-in directly to the harness, the Tarbuck Knot (Fig. 66A-B) remains a useful addition to the collection of general purpose knots. It's an adjustable loop. You can grasp the actual knot in your hand and slide it along the rope and it grips and holds under strain. It is a fine knot for tasks such as mooring small boats and improvising a tent, as long as lives do not depend on it.

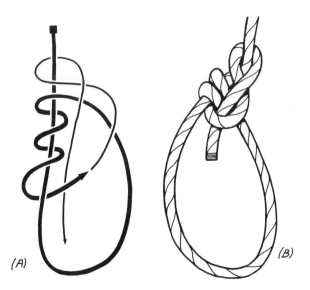

Fig. 66 Tarbuck Knot

Alpine Butterfly Knot (Fig. 67)

The Alpine Butterfly Knot is a picturesque name for what many climbers think is the best nonslip loop tied in the bight. It is a middleman's knot for climbers which fits around the chest and can be hauled from either direction. Note the crossing point where the bight emerges from the neck of the two interlocked loops (Fig. 67B). This is the hallmark of a properly made Alpine Butterfly Knot.

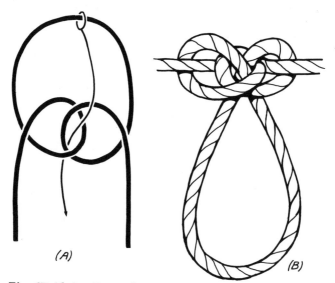

(A)   *(B)*

Fig. 67 Alpine Butterfly Knot

Manharness Hitch (Fig. 68)

Sometimes used as a middleman's tie-on, it seems to me that it lacks the proper stability for this important purpose, being designed to take the strain in one direction only. I suggest using it as a good general purpose knot. It's a very practical Loop Knot that you can tie quickly (Fig. 68A-B) in the bight. It can make a series of shoulder loops along a rope enabling people to pull a heavy load while their hands remain free. It was used to haul field guns into position (its other name being Artilleryman's Hitch); or to help horses (Harness Loop) when the going under foot was rough. Authorities agree that it's a one-way hitch, but nobody illustrates which way. I've always assumed it to be as shown (Fig. 68C). It's possible to middle a climbing rope, using a Manharness Hitch: Descend one part of the rope and then recover it by pulling on the other part (Fig. 68D-F).

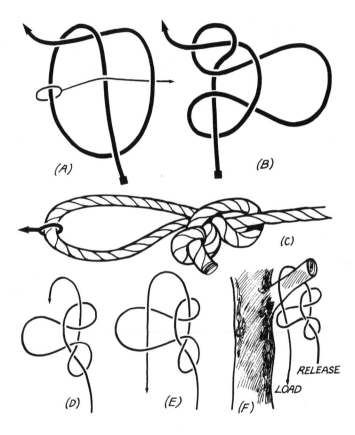

Fig. 68 Manharness Hitch

Frost Knot (Fig. 69)

The Frost Knot is just a simple Overhand or Thumb Knot tied in webbing.

A series of Frost Knots can be used (Fig. 69B) when tying webbing stirrups called "etriers," which take the form of a sort of improvised rope ladder.

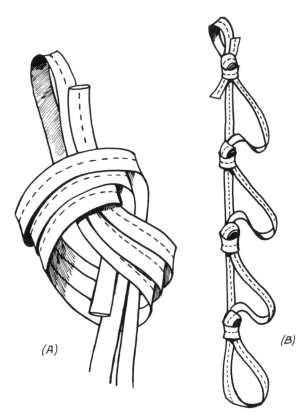

(A)

(B)

Fig. 69 Frost Knot

Figure of Eight Loop (Fig. 70)

A widely used fixed loop, this has many applications: It attaches a line to a carabiner (Fig. 70A-B). Or, using a bight as a working end pulled through the climber's waistband, the active rope may be anchored with an adaptation called an Anchor Knot (Fig. 70C). Its advantage over Alpine Butterfly Knots and other knots is its simplicity. It is unmistakable, and can be quickly checked. See Chapter 9—New Knots—for two variations. Three Quarter Figure of Eight Loops (Fig. 94) are worthy of consideration as alternatives.

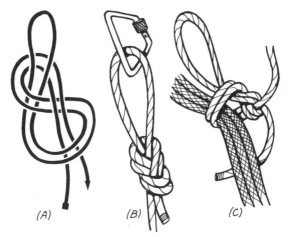

Fig. 70 Figure of Eight Loop

Bowline in the Bight (Fig. 71)

A reliable knot with a long history of sea use for rescue work or to sling an object, this knot forms two loops that do not slide. The secret of the Bowline in the Bight is that—although most parts of the knot are made in the doubled rope (Fig. 71A-B)—the bight around the standing parts is itself only single (Fig. 71C); and this single bight must be passed over the entire knot to complete the tying process.

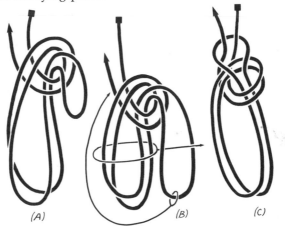

Fig. 71 Bowline in the Bight

Fireman's Chair Knot (Fig. 72)

This versatile rescue knot has been taught to fire brigades, the coast guards, mountain rescue teams, first aiders and many others engaged in emergency services. It is used to lift and lower from heights people who are unconscious, disabled or in danger, and it can be tied speedily in the bight.

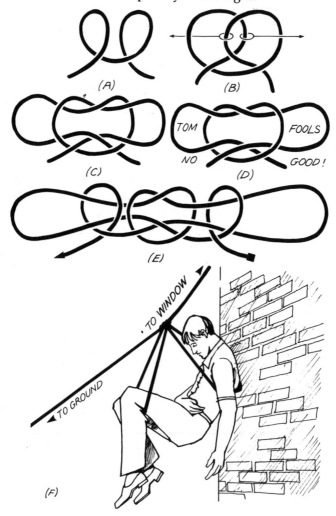

Fig. 72 Fireman's Chair Knot

Tie a Handcuff Knot (Fig. 72A-C). Do *not* use a Tom Fool's Knot, which occurs if the loops (Fig. 72B) are not interlaced correctly (Fig. 72D), for it is weaker. Slip one loop over the patient's head, around his or her back and under the armpits. The other loop goes around both legs behind the knees. Adjust them to size and lock each loop in place (Fig. 72E) with a Half Hitch. Then you can use the standing end of the rope to raise or lower the load, while a second person pulls the working end to keep the patient from bumping against walls, cliff faces, etc. (Fig. 72F). Most of these so-called "Handcuff Knots" were invented, I suspect, as leashes for animals. *Warning:* Unconscious patients are heavy, unmanageable and liable to fall out of any fixed loop knot to incur even more serious injury, unless you make sure each bight is tightened to grip the individual.

Triple Bowline (Fig. 73)

Tie a Bowline with a bight of line (make it with a doubled rope throughout, as in Fig. 73A: it is *not* a true Bowline in the bight). Draw the end of the bight downwards through the knot (Fig. 73B) to form a third loop. A useful variation, this is recommended for rescue and salvage purposes.

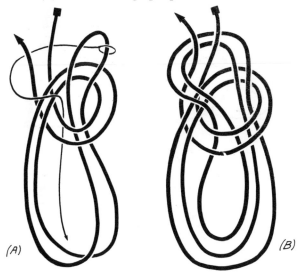

Fig. 73 Triple Bowline

Ontario Bowline (Fig. 74) and Algonquin Bowline (Fig. 75)

The Bowline (Fig. 13) and the Figure of Eight Loop (Fig. 70) tend to spill or drift, sometimes coming undone, if they cannot be fully tightened. These two loops (Figs. 74–75) seem to overcome that weakness in older, stiffer climbing ropes.

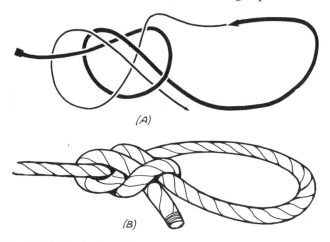

(A)

(B)

Fig. 74 Ontario Bowline

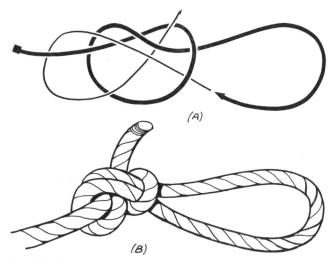

(A)

(B)

Fig. 75 Algonquin Bowline

One-Way Sheet Bend (Fig. 76)

The Common Sheet Bend (Fig. 14A) suffers from the disadvantage that one end sticks out more or less at right angles, with an increased chance that the knot may jam in a rocky crevice. Consider modifying the Sheet Bend (Fig. 76) so that both ends lie back away from the direction in which the rope is to be hauled. This could be a useful trick for hauling electric cables through cavity walls and beneath floorboards when rewiring the house.

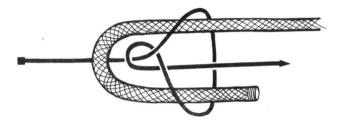

Fig. 76 One-Way Sheet Bend

8 • MISCELLANEOUS KNOTS

Heaving Line Knot (Fig. 77)

A heaving line is a light line which acts as a "messenger" (because it's sent on ahead) for a heavier line when it is thrown to a pier, or another vessel. The heavier line is then pulled across the gap. The end of the heaving line must be weighted to aid in the throwing. A climber may just add a snap-link to lob his line clear of a rocky ridge or crest. But, in boating circles, there's often someone waiting to catch the line, so the end must be soft. The Heaving Line Knot can, with practice, be set up in seconds (Fig. 77A-D)—and it won't hurt anyone.

Heaving lines will be about half-an-inch in diameter and up to 25 yards long. A flexible, braided texture is ideal. Boat heaving lines should float and be strong enough to tow a man through water.

Be sure to keep your end of a heaving line secure. It's not usual to bend it onto the heavier rope or cable before it's been thrown successfully. So, you may stand on the end or loop it around your wrist. One effective trick is to tuck a bight up inside your belt or climbing harness, pass the end through with a Figure of Eight Knot tied in it as a stopper, and draw the resulting Crossing Knot (Fig. 77E) snug. Do *not*, however, fasten yourself to a heaving line if there is any risk that you'll be hauled overboard, for example, by your craft overshooting its mooring or berth after the thrown end has been caught and secured.

Heaving Line Bend (Fig. 78)

You still need to bend your light messenger line to the heavy rope that will follow it. Sheet Bends and Double Sheet Bends (Fig. 14) are often impractical, because the sizes of the lines are too dissimilar (the thicker bight would straighten itself out, spilling the bend apart). A Racking Bend (Fig. 78), so-called because of its figure-of-eight (or "racking") seizing turns—which draw the sides of the thick bight together—is the solution.

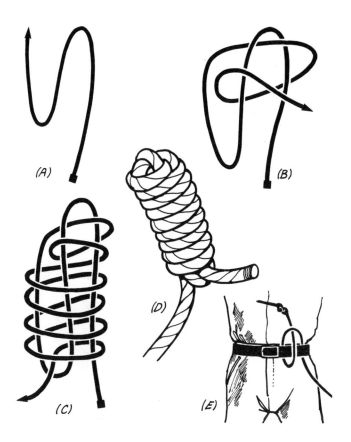

Fig. 77 Heaving Line Knot

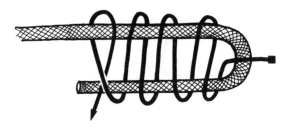

Fig. 78 Heaving Line Bend

Parbuckle (Fig. 79)

Recently I took delivery of an enormous piece of joinery weighing possibly 220 pounds. It was a flight of wooden steps, complete with handrails, custom built for my steeply terraced backyard. It was too big to go through any door. So, single-handed, using a ladder as an inclined ramp and a 2-inch hawser, I rolled it up and over my garage roof and lowered it triumphantly into the backyard. Mind you, before I got the hang of it, I nearly dropped it on the roof of my new car! The knot that did the trick was a Parbuckle.

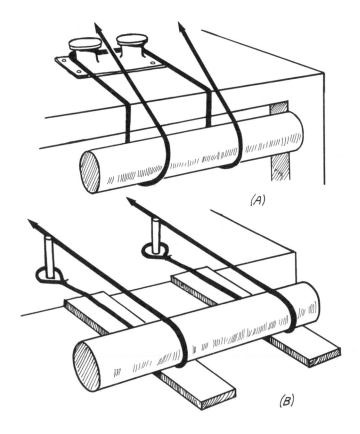

Fig. 79 Parbuckle

It works best with round objects (casks, kegs, logs, etc.), since there's very little friction as they roll with the movement of the rope. So almost all your effort is put to use. One person can do the work of two. A doubled line (Fig. 79A) is sufficient for short lengths of load. Longer loads need two separate lines (Fig. 79B). Guide and control the load with care, applying equal strain to each line or it may slip out of control.

Makeshift Knot (Fig. 80)

With this knot, even the weak can raise heavy loads. Even allowing for friction, the Makeshift Knot nearly doubles their pulling power. Don't stand beneath the load. Use a tough sling or strop; that's where the wear occurs. Reinforce the tree limb or other overhead support with burlap to minimize damage. To lift the load one yard, you'll need to pull down 2 yards of line.

Fig. 80 Makeshift Knot

First Aid

Bandages and slings should be tied off with Reef (or Square) Knots (Fig. 12), or, better still, a Reef Bow that can be undone easily without discomfort to the patient. Tie knots on the uninjured side, but be prepared to vary that rule to avoid patients having to lie upon knots. The Greeks and Romans used the Reef Knot to fix medical dressings as far back as 2,000 B.C. They believed wounds healed quicker if this knot was used. It seems that we're keeping the tradition, but have forgotten the reason.

Tying Packages (Fig. 81)

Anyone who ever worked in a shop in the days before adhesive tape and pre-packaged foods used to be expert at tying packages with string. Each purchase needed to be separately and speedily packed up for every customer. Children would watch amazed as the butcher or grocer, fingers moving faster than the eye could follow, formed and tightened knots without a pause in his conversation. The whole process was done automatically—quicker than thought!

Here's how they did it or, at least, one way. It works best with thin twine, and is a method worth learning.

(a) Pass the working end from your ball of twine under the packages, back across the top and then lead it around its standing part. Form a noose (Fig. 81A), leaving a generous tail end, which will be used to tie off later;

(b) Move the standing part backward and forward to tighten both the Slip Knot you've just tied and the grip of the twine around the package, until it holds firmly without any further help from you (Fig. 81B);

(c) Now make a trial pass with the twine around the package at right angles to the first part, decide how much more you'll need to finish, and cut it with some to spare;

(d) Make a second trip around the package, forming a Crossing Knot (Fig. 81C) for extra security at the back, and return to your original Slip Knot;

(e) To finish, take a Half Hitch around the first knot (Fig. 81D) and then use both ends of the string to tie half a Reef Knot on top. While thin twine will grip nicely, you might like to complete the Reef Knot for your own peace of mind.

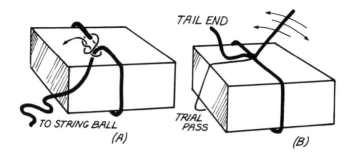

(A) TO STRING BALL

TAIL END

TRIAL PASS

(B)

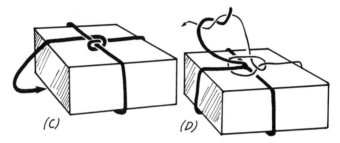

(C)

(D)

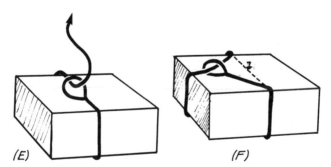

(E)

(F)

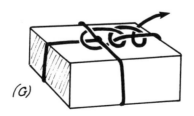

(G)

Fig. 81 Package Tying

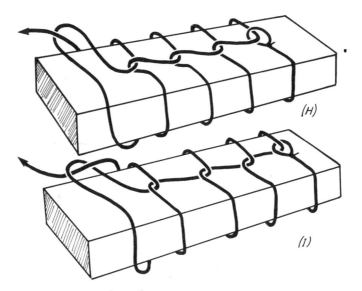

Fig. 81 (continued) Package Tying
(H) *Single Hitches.*
(I) *Marline Hitches.*

Tying Crates, Trunks and Other Large Loads

If you have to tie up crates, cabin trunks or other jumbo-sized loads, use thick cord—even rope if necessary—and use the following method to do the job:

Use a Running Bowline (Fig. 13D) or an Overhand Loop (Fig. 10C) or some other Packer's Knot (Fig. 19E-G) to make a loop and pass this around the crate (Fig. 81E). Lead the working end at right angles around one end of the crate, exerting sufficient tensions to pull the original turn around the crate into a slight "V" shape (Fig. 81F). On the reverse side of the crate (Fig. 81C) form a Crossing Knot (Fig. 19Q); and return to the start once more. Pull the "V" shape out straight with the final tuck of the string, which will tighten everything up nicely, and finish with a couple of Half Hitches (Fig. 81G).

Enclose long crates (Fig. 81H-I) with as many hitches as necessary, and a corresponding number of Crossing Knots (Fig. 19Q) on the reverse side. Use Single or Marline Hitches (see Fig. 40 for the difference).

Rope Ladder (Fig. 82)

This neatly knotted rope ladder (Fig. 82A-C) was first revealed in France at the beginning of the century as a boat's ladder for bathers. Each rung is just wide enough to insert one foot. Even then it uses a lot of line, so it's only right for a short ladder. Still, it's a handy idea to know. The upper bight is formed by a True Lover's Knot (Fig. 31).

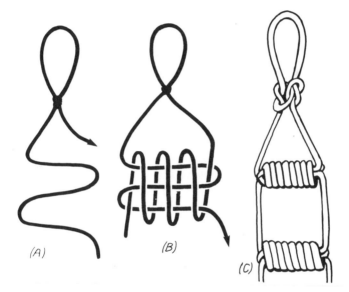

Fig. 82 Rope Ladder

Climbing Rope

To improvise a climbing rope which almost anyone could use in an emergency, tie a series of Alpine Butterfly Knots at conveniently spaced intervals. (See Fig. 67.)

Car Tow Ropes

The thicker your tow rope, the better. Sudden snatches can snap even the strongest ropes, especially if you've led them around sharp edges such as the inside of a bumper or a towing eye. Use nylon, which stretches. Protect it with sacking, where it is likely to chafe. *Note:* It's easier to bandage the rope with rags than to try to pad the bumper of the car.

To secure a tow rope, double a long bight which should be passed underneath the front of the vehicle and around the manufacturer's recommended anchor point on your vehicle. Pull out the bight until it is clear of the front bumper, headlights, license plate and other obstructions. Tie Julie's Hitch (Fig. 93) and secure the end to the standing part with a Bowline (Fig. 13). Julie's Hitch needs just one pass around the anchorage point, provides two loops as anchorage and enables all the knotting to be done with a clear view away from the car. The two turns that are the heart of the hitch absorb much of the strain of towing; one bight pulling into the other during sudden changes of direction can soak up further undesirable stresses within the hitch.

Vehicle Recovery (Fig. 83)

It's a helpless feeling to be stuck in your car in snow and mud. Pressing down on the accelerator and revving the engine only makes it worse. Going into second gear and revving the engine a few times—just enough to turn the car's wheels without stalling—is the right approach. Even then, you often need a helpful

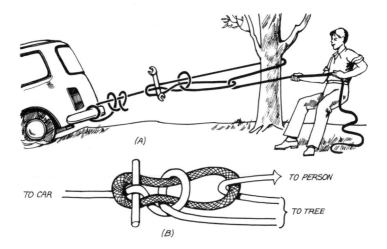

Fig. 83 Vehicle Recovery

push or pull applied at the same time. Solid ground and a grip for your tires may be only a yard or two away.

The Waggoner's Hitch (Fig. 21B), that modification of the Sheepshank (Fig. 21F), is a Makeshift Knot that can triple the pulling power. Tie your tow line securely to a firm anchorage point on the car. (Beware! You could easily pull off a bumper.) Use a Round Turn & Two Half Hitches (Fig. 17). "Dog" (see Glossary) one end of the Waggoner's Hitch (Fig. 83A) with a wrench or some other item from your toolbox. Lead the line's working end around that conveniently placed tree or lamppost, before passing it through the bight of the Waggoner's Hitch. No twist is required in the bight, as the loop is "dogged." Use rags, burlap or thick plastic sheets to pad the rope and protect the tree. Harsh wear on the bight can ruin that part of the rope, but in a crisis it may be worth it. A nice solution is to substitute a strop of stronger material for the bight (Fig. 83B).

Emergency Fan Belt
Never travel without a spare fan belt for your vehicle. However, you can improvise one. Use strong string or cord or tear up and roughly twist or plait together strips from a pair of tights, thin garden netting or some similar material. Wrap several turns around the pulley wheels involved—and that's the only trick, several turns rather than just one—before tying the ends tightly together with a Surgeon's Knot (Fig. 30). Drive gently and only as far as the next service station!

Split Hose Repairs
Leaking water hoses really need an adhesive bandage, but a tight whipping might just reduce a gush to a trickle if you're desperate. Constrictor Knots (Fig. 6) forcefully applied with the aid of pliers can hold just as well as a manufactured clip.

Luggage Rack Loads
It's against the law—and there's a heavy fine—for carrying a dangerously insecure load on your car's luggage rack. The knack of packing the load securely has little to do with the knots you choose. You may start with a Clove Hitch (Fig. 16) and finish off with a Round Turn & Two Half Hitches (Fig. 17), or use entirely

different knots. What is crucial is that you have the magination to foresee what could happen to your load during the journey should you be forced to brake, accelerate or turn a corner sharply. Obviously, it could shoot off the front, slide backwards, or roll off sideways. So, you need to tie it on so that none of those things can happen.

A small box may only need a couple of lashings across from side to side and another couple from front to back. Use separate short lengths. They're easier to tie and then, if one does work loose, the others will still be all right. Use flat tape or braid, which has more grip and will not put grooves in expensive suitcases or antique furniture. Swig each one tight (see "Swigging," page 43). An oar or canoe paddle or a length of copper piping for that do-it-yourself plumbing job will be secure with a couple of Transom Knots (Fig. 22), but a rolled-up carpet will need two separate lashings of some sort a long way apart.

Having made the load inseparable from the luggage rack, you have a new problem. The load may now pull the rack off the car. You may have to tie it onto the vehicle. Older cars used to have projecting door handles you could use as belaying points for this purpose. Modern cars have nothing, unless you wind down the windows and pass a line right through the inside of the car.

Water Knot (Fig. 84)

Hundreds of thousands of young swimmers train in schools and pools, and just as many swim for fun. Many of them now wear anti-chlorine goggles and, when the rubber headband breaks, it's difficult to tie the stretchy wet rubber straps together again. The best knot I've found to do it is—appropriately—the Water Knot. It grips securely; it's easy to tie and it doesn't use too much of the remaining strap.

Simply make an Overhand Knot (Fig. 84A) in one of the broken ends. Then insert the other end (Fig. 84B) and follow the knot around. Work the knot snug and tight (Fig. 84C) before putting the goggles back on.

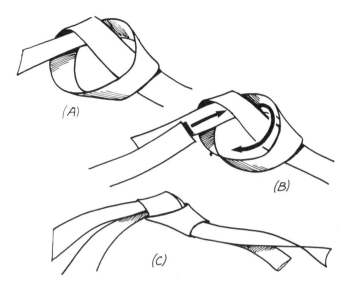

Fig. 84 Water Knot

9 ◆ NEW KNOTS

"Maybe the infant Raleigh, playing wistfully with string,
Took one more turn by accident, and stumbled on the thing."
—A. P. Herbert

Inventing a new knot is like discovering a new comet—it happens, but not often. Anyone can take a piece of line, make a few random tucks and come up with something that isn't in the knot books, calling it a new knot. To be any good and worth adopting, it should also be: (A) of some use, (B) as simple as possible, (C) easy to learn and tie, (D) easy to untie, (E) both strong and secure, and (F) distinctive and have a recognizable form. The knots which follow are all those things and—I believe—also relative newcomers on the knotting scene.

Rigger's (Hunter's) Bend (Fig. 85)

On Friday, October 6, 1978, the *London Times* carried a front page column 11 inches long reporting that retired consultant physician Dr. Edward Hunter had invented a new knot. In fact, he'd devised it some years earlier, but the media only then realized that it wasn't featured in the knotting literature. The media grabbed the story with enthusiasm. Dr. Hunter was interviewed on radio and TV. Knot-tying fans wrote in from Europe and America for more information.

Then, with publicity at its height, it was learned that an American, Phil D. Smith, had invented the knot in 1943 while he was employed on the San Francisco waterfront during World War II; he had actually published it in a booklet called "Knots for Mountaineers" in the 1950s. He had then described the knot as a Rigger's Bend.

Hunter's Bend (Fig. 85A)—as the knot is still known—is a strong, simple bend based on two interlocked Overhand Knots. British Royal Aircraft tested it to the breaking point in parachute cordage and found it ". . . not as strong as the Blood Knot (Fig.

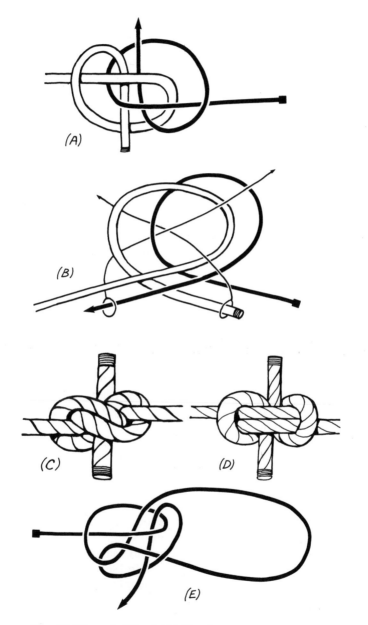

Fig. 85 Rigger's (Hunter's) Bend

44), similar to the reverse Figure of Eight (Fig. 28) and stronger than the Fisherman's Bend (Fig. 15), Sheet Bend (Fig. 14) or Reef Knot (Fig. 12)."

It's easy to tie. Holding both strands together and parallel, throw a loop (with no accidental crossovers, but keeping both strands parallel); then tuck each working end through the loop from opposite sides (Fig. 85B) and coax the knot into its final form (Fig. 85C—front view; Fig. 85D—rear view). You can even tie it as a Loop Knot (Fig. 85E).

Tumbling Thief Knot (center-tucked) (Fig. 86)

Desmond Mandeville of London is a prolific knot inventor. He has so many new knots to his credit that he has worked his way through the alphabet from "A" to "Z," giving them delightful names like Poor Man's Pride and Tumbling Thief.

The Common Thief Knot (Fig. 86A) resembles a Reef or Square Knot, but it distorts and slips in a totally unreliable way because its short ends are on opposite sides. Mr. Mandeville. found that when he loosened the knot and then crossed the ends over (Fig. 86B-C), he could persuade it to jam every time. Breaking it open by tugging one end away from the standing part of the rope, same as you'd capsize a Reef Knot into a Lark's Head Knot (Fig. 12E-F), caused a double tripping action (hence, the Tumbling Thief Knot). Not satisfied with a knot that only worked when coaxed carefully into shape, he went on to tuck each end in turn right through the center of the knot (Fig. 86D). The resulting new bend (Fig. 86E) is secure, strong and good looking. The unreliable thief has become respectable and taken up useful work as a bend to join large hawsers.

Poor Man's Pride (Fig. 87)

Knotting goes back so far in time it isn't surprising there's not much new to be discovered, but a lot also gets forgotten. Dr. Hunter shone a spotlight on Phil Smith's Rigger's Bend, which it hadn't had before (page 120). Desmond Mandeville found the Poor Man's Pride (Fig. 87A) for himself in 1961, and sent it to me for scrutiny during all the excitement over Hunter's Bend. It took about a year to uncover the truth. It's really the Rosendahl Bend (otherwise known as the Zeppelin Knot), named after Charles Rosendahl, commander of the U.S. airship *Los Angeles*, who apparently insisted his craft be moored with this bend. That was back in the 1930s, when it was claimed to be superior to the Carrick Bend (Fig. 29), Bowline (Fig. 13) or Sheet Bend (Fig. 14), and always quick to untie. One snag with Commander Rosendahl's favorite bend seemed to be that we couldn't tie it as slickly as Hunter's Bend, until Ettrick Thomson of Suffolk came up with a very neat solution (Fig. 87B-D).

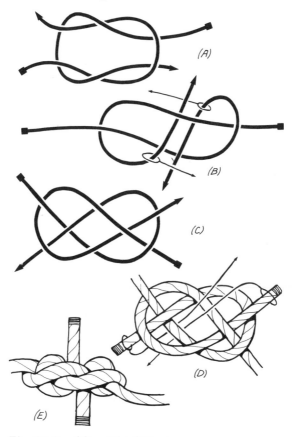

Fig. 86 Tumbling Thief Knot
(A) Thief Knot.
(B) Thief Knot with ends crossed over.
(C) Tumbling Thief Knot.
(D)-(E) Tumbling Thief Knot (center-tucked).

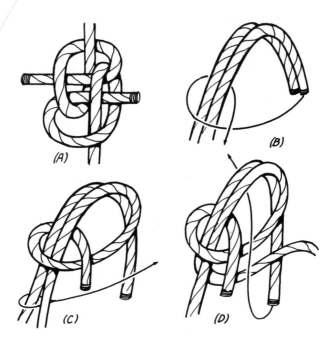

Fig. 87 Poor Man's Pride

Bend "X" (Fig. 88)

This is another of Desmond Mandeville's ideas. It can either be used to shorten ropes or as a tensioning device, and is easy to adjust. Unlike the Sheepshank, it cannot fall apart, but it needs working ends which the Sheepshank, being tied in the bight, does not.

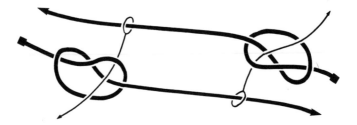

Fig. 88 Bend "X"

Release Hitches (Figs. 89–90)

Canadian Bob Chisnall is an experienced mountaineer who, very sensibly, is concerned with finding the best knots for climbing. He devised these Release Hitches to overcome the shortcomings of other Prusik-type knots (Figs. 61, 64, 65). It is suggested that Release Hitches properly used should reduce the chances of accidents considerably.

Release Hitches (Figs. 89–90) have two ends, a load end and a release end (Figs. 89B–90B). The load end of the knot runs from the usual set of turns wrapped around the rappel line, and any loading of this end naturally causes the knot to grip the line. The release end runs parallel to the rappel line, and is contained by each wrap of the knot. Once jammed, the knot is released with a sharp tug on the release end. This tug causes the uppermost wrap to slip, and it in turn causes the one below it to slide. This action is spread down through the series of coils or wraps until each one is freed and the knot slides.

These Release Hitches (Figs. 89–90) have advantages and disadvantages. The first Release Hitch (bottom-load version, Fig. 89A-B) is more secure than the Prusik Knot and it will grip even when sloppily tied, but it tends to drift apart when loaded if there's any slack. Then you have to tug very hard on the release end to get it to slip. When tied neatly, bottom-load Release Hitches like this one can be freed easily. The second Release Hitch (top-loaded, Fig. 90A-B) is just the opposite. If the knot is the least bit sloppy or loose, it will slide before jamming, or it may even fail. If it is not snug, it will slide several feet as it is tightened before coming to rest. However, it releases readily.

Adjustable Knot (Fig. 91)

The practical experience of Bob Chisnall is evident, once again, in this excellent slide-and-lock knot. The Adjustable Loop (Fig. 91A) will slide easily in either direction, but it locks up firmly under a load. After release of the load you can once again slide it along the rope. Two of the knots will make an Adjustable Bend (Fig. 91B); and, in a single piece of line, this would create an Adjustable Strop or Sling (Fig. 91C).

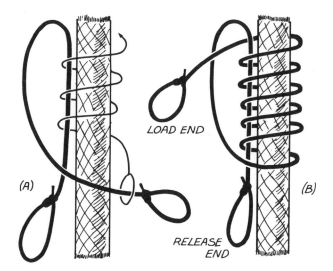

Fig. 89 Release Hitch (Bottom Load)

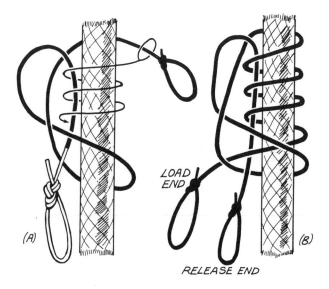

Fig. 90 Release Hitch (Top Load)

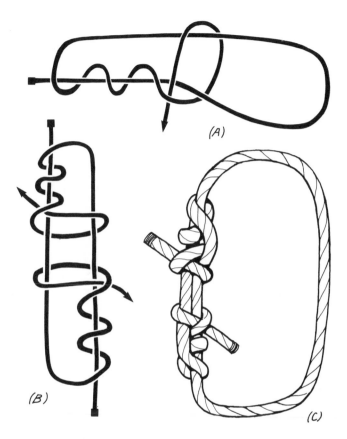

Fig. 91 Adjustable Knot

Vibration-Proof Hitch (Fig. 92)

This interesting idea came from Amory Bloch Lovins. He's the one who pointed out that the Hunter's Bend (Fig. 85) was actually Phil Smith's Rigger's Bend. Mr. Lovins, after 12 years as a guide in the White Mountains of New Hampshire and teaching woodcraft in Maine, had certainly picked up some knots and tying methods that were new to me. His Vibration-Proof Hitch lays up well (Fig. 92A-C) only if the spar around which it is formed is fairly large in relation to the diameter of the line. Then vibration by anything attached to the standing part (a flapping sail, for instance) will only tighten it, owing to a double ratchet action within the knot parts.

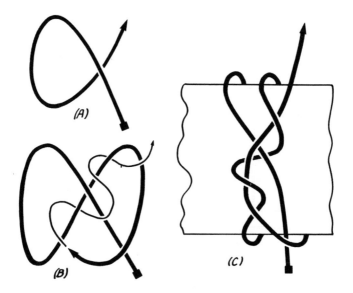

Fig. 92 Vibration-Proof Hitch

Julie's Hitch (Fig. 93)

In 1974, my younger daughter Julie—who was then 9 years old—invented this knot (Fig. 93A-C) herself. It is stable, easy to learn and seems original. With a couple of adjustments you can enlarge or make smaller both loops, and you can enlarge one of the two splayed bights at the expense of the other. There is an excellent practical use for it: attaching tow ropes to broken down vehicles (see car tow ropes, page 115). *Note:* the working end must be attached to the standing part with a Bowline (Fig. 93D).

Three-Quarter Figure of Eight Loops (Fig. 94)

These two variations (Fig. 94A-B) of the Figure of Eight Loop (Fig. 70) so popular with climbers these days, have the advantage that the ends can be pulled in opposite directions—a situation which is often necessary—without distorting the knots.

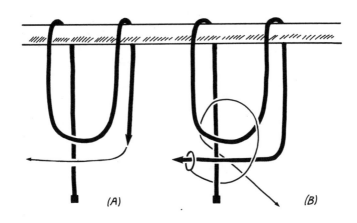

(A)

(B)

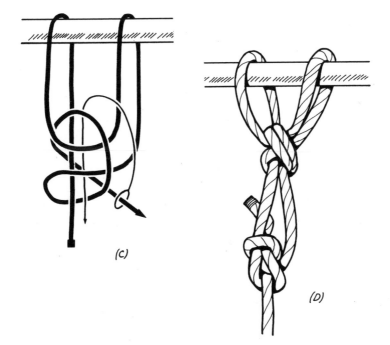

(C)

(D)

Fig. 93 Julie's Hitch
Secure the working end to the standing part with a Bowline.

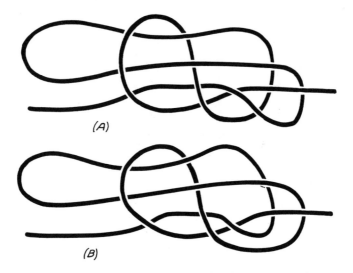

(A)

(B)

Fig. 94 Three-Quarter Figure of Eight Loops

10 ♦ TRICKS

The best string tricks work like magic every time, without any special skill or preparation. Many of those I've chosen cannot fail to puzzle onlookers of any age, but the real test is whether you can use them to amuse young children at parties. I believe the following will work for you—they do for me.

INTERLOCKING HANDCUFFS (Fig. 95)

Attention, party organizers! Bowlines (Fig. 13) can be used for make-belief handcuffs. They needn't be tight. You can link two volunteers together (Fig. 95A) and then challenge them to separate without either cutting the line, untying the knots or slipping the loops off their wrists.

Young children love it; and, with very little encouragement, will climb in and out of the large bights and turn somersaults through each other's arms in ingenious efforts to free themselves (allow about 1½ yards for each line to permit these antics). Onlookers will find it fun. It can be an ice-breaker at adult parties, too.

The solution—passing a bight under one wrist loop (Fig. 95B) and then over the hand of the captive—is even funnier for being so unspectacular.

OVERHAND KNOTS GALORE (Fig. 96)

I like this one because it's the nearest to magician's sleight of hand I can achieve—but it's really very easy. Build up a series of Half Hitches on your thumb (Fig. 96A) until it's full (the thinner the cord, the more Half Hitches, and the better the impression). Trap the working end on top of your thumb with a finger. Carefully draw all those Half Hitches off your thumb (Fig. 96B), and at the same time carry that trapped end through the tunnel formed by the Half Hitches until it comes out at the other end.

Now transfer the bunched-up bird's nest of half-formed knots gently into the palm of your hand, surrounding it with your fingers so that only the arrowed end sticks up out of your grasp. Take that end between the fingers of your free hand and steadily draw it out. Overhand knots will appear (Fig. 96C), neatly spaced, one after the other. If at any time you sense a slight snag within the remaining concealed Half Hitches, which could develop into a hopeless tangle, manipulation with your fingers will resolve it. Tell some far-fetched yarn as you tie the knots, such as how you became the Knotting Champion of the World.

Fig. 95 Interlocked Handcuffs

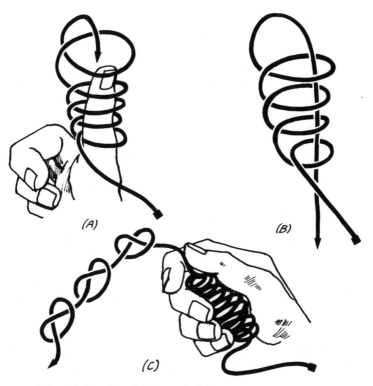

Fig. 96 Overhand Knots Galore

RELEASING THE SCISSORS (Fig. 97)

Many knotted string release tricks are based upon the principle of drawing slack out of a hitch, and passing the bight obtained over the object to be freed. It works with rings, keys and buttonholes. Scissors have the seemingly added complication of the line passing through the fingerholds. It makes no difference. The challenge is always to free the item—whatever it is—without touching the free ends of the string.

THREADING THE NEEDLE (Fig. 98)

This clever little illusion cannot fail to outwit your audience. Show a small bight of cord between finger and thumb, with your other hand pointing the free end of the cord at the bight and attempting to poke it through (Fig. 98A) as if you're threading a needle. Explain that you will get it through the loop without letting go of the end, although the loop is obviously too small to get your hand through.

Then add that, "to make it even harder" you will alter the set-up slightly. Take a great many turns around your thumb before you form the bight (Fig. 98B). Pick up the end again and—after a few practice passes—suddenly dart your hand forward, passing it to the side of the bight by the end of your thumb. Loosen your grip on the bight momentarily, letting the cord slip around the end of your thumb and into the bight from below. The back of your hand and fingers will mask this, and besides, it occurs too fast for the unprepared eye to follow. Your audience will see the end threaded through the bight, still in your hand, but will fail to notice that the bight has reversed itself and that one of the turns around your thumb has vanished (Fig. 98C).

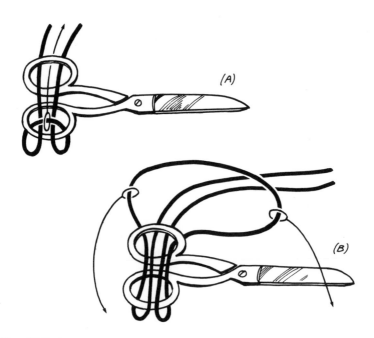

Fig. 97 Releasing the Scissors

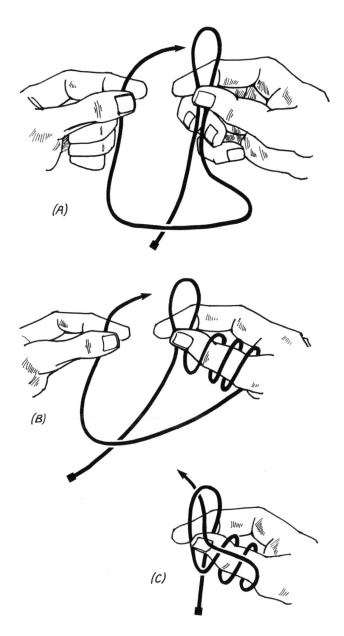

Fig. 98 Threading the Needle

UNFOLDING A KNOT (Fig. 99)

Not for an adult audience, this will intrigue small children. Lay out a length of string, or a table napkin. The trick is to hold one end in each hand and then to tie a knot without letting go of the ends. The solution is to fold your arms (Fig. 99A), which ties them in a knot, before you pick up the ends. Then, as you unfold your arms, you transfer the Overhand Knot that they formed to the string or napkin (Fig. 99B).

Fig. 99 Unfolding a Knot

A DISAPPEARING KNOT (Fig. 100)

Loosely, and with great deliberation, demonstrate tying the two halves of a Reef Knot (Fig. 100A). Then interweave and tuck (Fig. 100B) one of the working ends even more "to make it really secure." Keep the creation loose. Although it looks complicated, a steady pull on the ends will cause it to fall apart, leaving the cord unknotted once again.

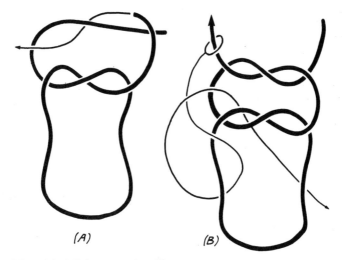

Fig. 100 A Disappearing Knot

THE WORLD'S WORST KNOT (Fig. 101)

This bend (Fig. 101A-B) is a combination of the Thief Knot and the Granny Knot with the weaknesses of both, so it slips and slides with little chance of it jamming at all. Perhaps it should be called a "G-Reef" Knot, for whoever tries to hold anything with it would soon come to grief! Tied in two smooth and flexible cords, it can be made to travel steadily down both lines by pulling them apart (Fig. 101C-E). The tuck is particularly effective if you use different colored cords. Watch the two parts of the line that come from the underside of the knot. If they change places (Fig. 101F), the knot will jam and the tuck won't work. Prevent it from happening by standing with one foot casually placed on a box or step, with your thigh raised, and one line hanging down on either side of your leg. Giving each end a slight twist with your fingers (experience will quickly show which way) also helps. If the knot does jam, just pass the cords to one of your audience, asking that the demonstration continue. Then you can blame that poor innocent bystander for what has gone wrong with the knot!

(A)   (B)

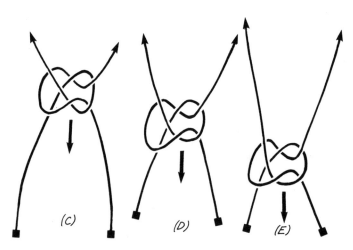

(C)   (D)   (E)

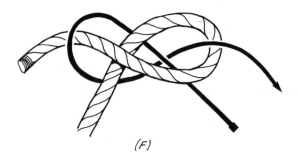

(F)

Fig. 101 The World's Worst Knot

FIND THE MIDDLE (Fig. 102)

This gimmick has been operated for centuries by carnival swindlers to separate their victims from their money. It works best with a man's leather belt.

Double the belt in half, forming a tight loop in the middle; then roll it up snugly and hold it on a flat surface. Note that two identical tear-shaped spaces have been created at the center of the roll. One is, of course, the loop in the middle of the belt, but the closer you study the spaces, the harder it is to be sure which it really is (*Note:* be sure *not* to use a belt with distinctive light and dark sides, or patterned and plain, for this will give away the trick to a quick, calculating mind.)

Invite your victim to insert a pencil or something else with a point into the loop formed at the middle of the belt. If he chooses the right space, when you pull away the ends of the belt his pencil should trap the belt by the loop. If wrong, the belt will slip around it and remain free.

But—here's how you, the operator, can win every time. First, *you* must be sure which space is the real loop! Second, you vary the routine imperceptibly depending upon which selection your victims make. Should they choose the wrong space (Fig. 102B), no problem: Just pull both ends away together. But if they select the right loop (Fig. 102A), then defeat them by taking the outer end and pulling the two ends away in opposite directions, as shown in Fig. 102B.

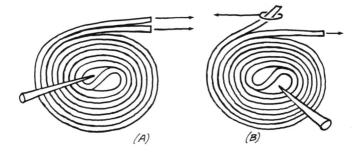

Fig. 102 Find the Middle

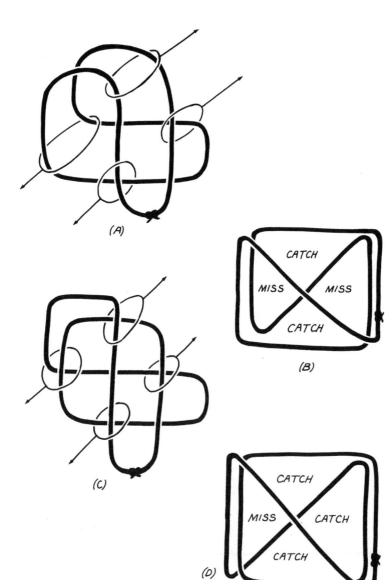

Fig. 103 The Finger Trap

THE FINGER TRAP (Fig. 103)

Toss a knotted cord onto the table (Fig. 103A-B) casually, and deftly spread it into the rectangular form. (A small, flexible metal chain or necklace works well.) Invite an onlooker to place his or her finger in any one of the four triangular compartments. Then neatly pull the string away. If it slides around the finger, without trapping it, the onlooker wins. If it snags around the finger, you—the operator—win. There are two positions in which the finger would be caught and two in which the string would be released. So there's a 50/50 chance, a genuine even-money bet, with onlooker and operator taking equal risks of winning or losing. Right? Wrong!

This is another of those swindles adopted by the street people and carnival sharks, because the percentages can be switched in their favor. How is it done?

With an unnoticed twist of the wrist, just before the downward pointing loop is laid over the sideways one, you can throw down the cord in a different layout (Fig. 103C-D) which you can quickly spread so that it looks exactly like the first game. Notice, however, that there are now three places where you can win, compared with only one for the poor old onlooker. Just as your audience begins to get the hang of it, at least one of the compartments changes its nature to catch or release! Played for money in a public place this could get you arrested, but played privately among friends—for pennies or matches—it can bring some hilarious moments.

FREE THE RING (Fig. 104)

The hand is quicker than the eye in this simple manipulation, which takes a little practice. Pass the endless loop through a ring (Fig. 104A). It works just as well with scissors, a key, or someone's buttonhole. Suspend the loop on both thumbs as shown, and then pick up a bight with each little finger in turn, exactly as shown (Fig. 104B). Cast off the loop from the little finger of your left hand and, at the same moment, cast off the loop from the thumb of your right hand—pull your hands apart swiftly. Faster than onlookers can see or understand, the ring will drop from the cord as if it has been cut in two.

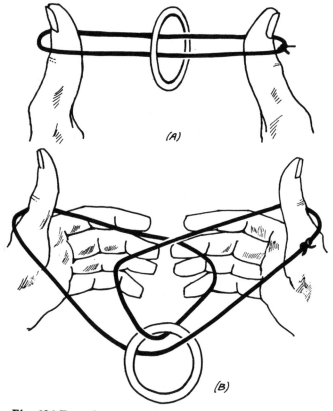

(A)

(B)

Fig. 104 Free the Ring

CUTTING AND RESTORING ROPE (Fig. 105)

Double a piece of cord, cut the loop you've made with scissors or a knife—and seconds later let the audience examine the same piece of cord. It has been rejoined magically!

This is a classic illusion, and professional magicians have evolved over 100 ways to present it. Just as you think you've figured out how it's done, they switch to another method. Some use gimmicky ropes with concealed fastenings. Others depend upon sleight-of-hand to palm spare sliding knots. Occasionally, it can be done only on-stage.

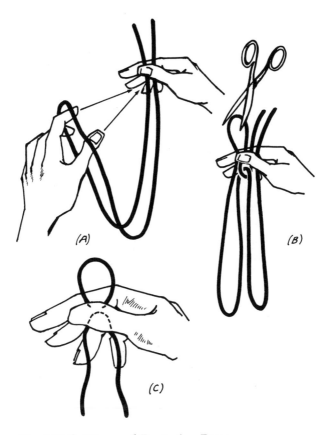

Fig. 105 Cutting and Restoring Rope

I can survive happily with young audiences on just two of the straightforward versions which need no special skill or preparation; these follow.

Method #1: Display an intact piece of magician's cord (white cotton braided rope or a synthetic fiber equivalent) about two yards long. Double it, explaining that you need to find the exact center of the line, and hold the two ends close together, pointing upwards, between thumb and fingers—with the back of your hand towards your audience (you are going to do something behind that hand that you don't want them to see). Locate the middle of the cord as it dangles down in front of you and pick up the bight over your free thumb and finger (Fig. 105A). Then, as far as anyone can tell, you place the bight forming the middle of the cord beside the two short ends poking up that are already in full view. *Actually*—surreptitiously (and in a smooth uninterrupted pass of your hand)—you pick up a part of the cord *below* one of the short ends . . . and form this into a visible bight (Fig. 105B), which now appears to be the middle of the rope. What you have just done should be completely masked by your innocent hand holding up the ends.

Cut the line, claiming you are cutting it in half, although really you are only snipping off an inch or so at one end. The rest is showmanship. You may lick the cut ends (magic glue!) and then tuck them down into your fist to be sealed back together, or sprinkle invisible sticky dust over them and mutter incantations. Suddenly, toss the intact line out into your audience for inspection. Focusing on the flying line will take their eyes away from you as you pocket that short snip of cord, or deposit it in a nearby vase.

Once is never sufficient for this trick. You must repeat it. Having shown clearly the first time that you had nothing concealed in your hands, you can safely retain that snip left over from the first cut to use in version number two.

Method #2: This time, to squelch the suspicion of those who wonder why you held the cord in such a peculiar way before, simply pick up the cord by its approximate middle (with the ends dángling down) and place it directly in your other hand with the bight showing. Only, once again, it's a false bight (Fig. 105C). You've bent that snip of cord over into an upside-down "U" shape and that's what the audience sees.

Cut it, throw out the rope for inspection, and dispose of the two smaller snips. *Note:* Since the line loses an inch or more each time you cut, you'll need about two yards for the missing portions to go unnoticed.

Glossary

GLOSSARY

Abseil—the act of riding down an anchored climbing rope in a self-controlled descent (also called "rappelling").

Anchor—quite apart from its usual meaning, the term "anchor" used in regard to knotting rope (particularly climbers' ropes) means "belaying" (see below) for safety purposes.

Barrel Knot—see "Blood Knot."

Belay—to wind a rope under load in a figure-of-eight pattern around a fixture to make the rope fast. Climbers use the term somewhat differently; for them belaying is protecting or controlling themselves with a safety line.

Bend—a knot which ties the ends of two free ropes together, or the action of knotting two ropes together (same origin as the word "bind").

Bight—the slack part of a rope between either end and the standing part, particularly when it forms a loop or partial loop. Knots tied "in the bight" or "on the bight" do not need the ends for the tying process.

Blood Knot (or Barrel Knot)—any one of a group of knots, used especially by anglers, with numerous wrapping turns (giving them a barrel-shaped appearance) to keep a relatively high breaking strength.

Breaking Strength—an estimation of the load that will cause a rope to part, as calculated by manufacturers. It does not take into account wear and tear, shock-loading or weakening by knotting, and is not the safe working load (also see "Safe Working Load").

Cable—any large rope or anchor warp (or chain) is called a cable; but "cable-laid" rope is three right-handed hawsers laid up left-handed to form a larger 9-strand rope or cable.

Capsize—to distort a knot by tugging or overloading it so that it loses its characteristic layout. It may be a fault that causes the knot to weaken or spill apart, but you can also capsize some knots deliberately as a quick way of tying or untying them.

Carabiner—a metal snap-link used by climbers as an attachment for ropes.

Cord—strictly speaking, cord is made up of several tightly twisted yarns that make a small line under 10 mm in diameter; but "cordage" is a comprehensive word for any line, whatever its size or material, which has no special purpose.

Core—the loosely twisted strand, or bundle of parallel yarns or filaments, running the length of larger ropes to form an inner heart or filler. Found in ropes of more than three strands and in most braided lines, it may be simply a cheap filler of weak stuff; or it could have a specific role as a stiffener or reinforcer.

Dog—to wind the tail end of a rope back several times around itself or another rope (often larger), with the lay, and secure it temporarily against a lengthwise pull. A draw-loop also may be said to be "dogged" when you prevent it from undoing accidentally, either by whipping it or by poking something through it.

Eight Plait—rope of the larger sizes made up of four pairs of strands, two spiralling clockwise and two counter-clockwise; it is strong but flexible and will not kink.

End—usually the end of line which is being knotted, whipped, etc., more precisely called the "running end," "working end" or "free end" (see also "Standing End").

Eye—a loop usually made in the end of rope by splicing it.

Fiber—the natural vegetable equivalent of filaments; the smallest element of rope construction, which is twisted to make yarns.

Filament—the smallest element of material forming the individual fibers of synthetic rope.

Hard Laid—tightly twisted rope.

Hawser—strictly speaking, any very large rope over about 1.6 inches in diameter which is not a cable, but which is big enough for towing or mooring. It is generally used to refer to all 3-strand right-handed ropes.

Heart—see "Core."

Hitch—a knot that secures a rope to a post, ring, spar or rail, etc., or to another rope which takes no part in tying the knot. It won't keep its shape on its own. In climbers' jargon, a "hitch" is often just a temporary fastening.

Kernmantel Rope—sheath and core climbers' rope designed to absorb shock elastically.

Knot—the word is used to cover every kind of occasion where the end of a line is passed through a loop in itself. But, strictly speaking, "Knots" are also considered to be a special category separate from "bends" and "hitches," which consists of only: (a) Binding Knots, (b) Stopper Knots in the end of line, (c) knots forming loops or nooses and (d) knots joining small lines together (usually referred to as bends), or joining both ends of the same small line.

Lanyard—a small line, often braided and ornamental, attached to knives and other personal items to prevent your losing them; also a line used to secure and tighten rigging on sailing vessels.

Lay—the direction, either left-handed or right-handed, of twist in the strands of rope; also the nature (tight, medium or loose) of that twist.

Lead—the direction taken by the working end through any knot, giving an indication of how it was tied, or of a rope around an object.

Line—a general label for most cordage with no special purpose. It is also used to refer to rope that does have a purpose, such as clothesline, heaving line, fishing line.

Loop—a part of the rope that is bent so that its parts come together or actually cross.

Make Fast—to secure a rope with a hitch, or to belay (also see "Belay").
Messenger—a light line passed or thrown over a gap in advance of a heavier rope, etc., which it will then haul or hoist across the gap.
Middle—to fold a line into two equal parts to locate the center.

Natural Rope—cordage of all kinds made from vegetable fibers.
Nip—the binding, frictional pressure within a knot that prevents it from slipping; a sharp turn in a rope creating the point in a knot where parts grip each other.
Noose—a loop secured around its own standing part to create a slip knot which pulls tight.

Parbuckle—an arrangement of the ends of a single rope around a cylindrical object so as to lift or lower it through a rolling movement.

Rappel—see "Abseil."
Reef—shortening a sail (reducing its surface area, for instance, to cope with strengthening winds), which is traditionally achieved by bunching the sail and parcelling it up at intervals with short lengths of line sewn onto the sail at regular points—using Reef Knots.
Reeve—to pass the end of a rope through any opening, as you do, when making up a block and tackle.
Rope—any cordage over .4 inch in diameter.

"S" Laid Rope—left-handed rope.
Safe Working Load—the estimated load which can be placed upon a rope without it breaking, taking account of its age, condition, the knots used and the possibility of shock-loading. The safe working load may be as little as one-sixth the rope's breaking strength (also see "Breaking Strength").
Security—a knot's inherent ability to resist slipping, distorting or capsizing under a load or intermittent jerking. This quality is quite distinct from "Strength" (also see "Strength").

Sling—rope, wire or webbing put around an object, usually in the form of an endless band (best spliced but sometimes knotted), to hoist or haul it; often called a "Strop" (also see "Strop"). Climbers may call an extra loop attachment for their climbing ropes a sling.

Small Stuff—line under .4 inch in diameter, but especially cord, string, thread, etc.

Soft Laid—loosely twisted rope.

Standing End—the opposite end to the working end (also see "End").

Standing Part—the part of a rope not being handled or worked, as opposed to the ends or a bight.

Staple—graded fibers or chopped filaments for ropemaking (rope made from staple has a fibrous or fuzzy surface due to all the ends).

Strand—yarns twisted together in the opposite direction to that of the yarn itself, a major element in the complete rope. Rope made with strands—not braided—is "laid line." "Stranded" rope has one strand broken or severely damaged.

Strength—the knot's capacity to withstand a load without breaking the line. It is distinctly different from "Security" (also see "Security").

String—thick thread, twine, thin cordage, usually for home use.

Strop—strictly speaking, the rope or wire band (or strap) seized around a pulley block to suspend it; the word is often used for a "Sling" (also see "Sling").

Synthetic Rope—rope made from man-made filaments or staples.

Taking a Turn—leading a rope around a post or some other fixing for friction prior to belaying.

Thread—a yarn; otherwise, fine line for sewing.

Warp—to move a vessel by means of hawsers. Warps may be hawsers used for that purpose or mooring lines. Weavers' warps are the threads running lengthwise in weaving.

Weft—the transverse weaving threads.

Whipping—the tight wrapping of the end of a rope with small stuff to prevent it unlaying and fraying.

Working End—see "End."

Yarn—any number of individual fibers or filaments twisted together as the first stage in ropemaking.

"Z" Laid Rope—right-handed rope.

Index

The International Guild of Knot Tyers

The Guild grew from an idea by Des Pawson, a British knot craftsman, and the author. At the inaugural meeting aboard the Maritime Trust's vessel R.R.S. *Discovery* in April, 1982, twenty-five founder members voted unanimously to create the international guild, appointing a steering committee and agreeing to constitutional rules, membership conditions, etc.

The Guild's objects are ". . . to promote the art, craft and science of knotting, its study and practice; to undertake research into all aspects of knotting; and to establish an authoritative body for consultative purposes."

Membership is open to anyone interested in knotting (whether expert or simply hoping to learn from others) and has grown fast to include established authors and consultants of knotting, sail-makers and bell-rope tyers, Sea Scouts and Rangers, boat owners, in the U.K., the U.S.A., Australia, Europe and Asia.

The members keep in touch through a quarterly newsletter and a couple of meetings a year, but regional groups may meet more often. The annual subscription is modest, aiming simply to cover costs.

If you'd like to know more, contact the Guild's Hon. Secretary, Geoffrey Budworth, 45 Stambourne Way, Upper Norwood, London, England SE19 2PY.